Hold Your Audience

William J. McCullough has, since 1941, lectured on effective speaking at eleven colleges, provided instructional programs for industry and civil service, conducted methods of instruction courses for the U.S. Army, and directed Dale Carnegie classes in New York, New Jersey, and Georgia. He has had experience on the stage, on television, and in motion pictures. He is President of Looseleaf Law Publications, Inc. and Modern Promotions Courses, Inc.

Hold Your Audience

The Way to Success in Public Speaking

William J. McCullough

A SPECTRUM BOOK

Prentice-Hall, Inc., Englewood Cliffs, N.J. 07632

Library of Congress Cataloging in Publication Data

McCULLOUGH, WILLIAM J.
   Hold your audience.

   (A Spectrum Book)
   Includes index.
   1. Public speaking. I. Title.
PN4121.M245   808.5'1   77-27840
ISBN 0-13-392555-2
ISBN 0-13-392548-X pbk.

A Spectrum Book

Printed in the United States of America

10   9   8   7   6   5   4   3   2   1

PRENTICE-HALL INTERNATIONAL, INC., *London*
PRENTICE-HALL OF AUSTRALIA PTY., LIMITED, *Sydney*
PRENTICE-HALL OF CANADA, LTD., *Toronto*
PRENTICE-HALL OF INDIA PRIVATE, LIMITED, *New Delhi*
PRENTICE-HALL OF JAPAN, INC., *Tokyo*
PRENTICE-HALL OF SOUTHEAST ASIA PTE., LTD., *Singapore*
WHITEHALL BOOKS, LIMITED, *Wellington, New Zealand*

Contents

Introduction

The greatest military invasion in history took place on June 6, 1944. On its twentieth anniversary, General Eisenhower was describing this amphibious operation carried out under his command. He recalled, "Our men were tied down on the beach. There was confusion, there was congestion. Then someone said, 'Let's get out of here,' and the breakthrough into France was on."

That someone supplied a timely bit of effective speaking. Those five words triggered the action that turned the tide of battle. That enterprising someone recognized the need, accepted the opportunity to speak, and spoke.

HOW DO YOU FEEL
ABOUT SPEAKING TO AN AUDIENCE?

Somewhere, at this moment, somebody is speaking to an audience because he or she *wants* to speak. Conversely, somewhere at this moment, somebody is dying a thousand deaths because he or she *does not want* to speak before an audience but is required to do so. How about you? Into which category do you fall?

Do you *welcome the opportunity* to occupy the speaker's platform? (You should, and you're going to find out why you should in the pages that follow.)

While you deliver a speech, do you *enjoy* being before the audience? (If not, this book will help you.)

After you finish a speech, do you feel a *sense of satisfaction and accomplishment?* (This text explores the reasons why some speakers fail and others succeed in achieving their goals.)

THE CONTENT OF THIS BOOK

Now that we have made these seemingly extravagant claims concerning the potential of this text, it seems appropriate that we should spell out how we plan to proceed.

We will define and explain the fundamentals of effective speaking by considering five principal areas:

1. The *musts*. These are the elements the speaker *must* include if the speech is to succeed.
2. The *don't worries*. These are items that seem to be important troublemakers. Actually, they shouldn't cause you any concern.
3. The *helps*. These are the highly desirable qualities that make positive contributions to the good speech.
4. The *avoids*. These are the negative characteristics that should not be included in your speech.
5. After you read and digest the *musts, don't worries, helps,* and *avoids,* you will be ready to

begin your own *personal* development program. Therefore, in this fifth area we discuss a plan for your speech-making future entitled, "How to Improve." By adopting the proper attitude and by following practical guidelines, you will be on your way toward becoming a more effective speaker.

one
The
"Musts"
of Effective
Speaking

A few years ago I visited the 92nd Police Precinct in Brooklyn. As I entered, the desk officer looked at me and shouted "Stop!" He was in uniform with a gun, so I stopped. He raised his arm in my direction and said slowly, "Knowledge, sincerity, enthusiasm, practice." I walked up to the desk, shook the lieutenant's hand, and said, "Thank you very much."

THE MEANING OF "MUSTS"

Three years earlier, that desk officer had heard me give a series of lectures on effective speaking. I said to the audience, "If you forget everything else we have talked about but you remember the four *musts* of effective speaking, then our time together will have been well spent." When the lieutenant repeated "Knowledge, sincerity, enthusiasm, and practice," he proved that our classroom encounter was a success and I was grateful.

Very briefly, here is what the four *musts* denote:

Knowledge — You *must* know your subject.
Sincerity   — You *must* believe in your subject.
Enthusiasm— You *must* be eager to tell about it.
Practice   — You *must* speak, at every opportunity.

Now that we have introduced the *must* family, let's examine each one in depth.

KNOWLEDGE

More than two hundred years ago, Alexander Pope wrote his *Essay on Criticism*. In this classic work he stated, "A little knowledge is a dangerous thing; drink deep or drink not from the Peirian spring." This theme should be applied to a speaking effort. If you go in front of an audience with insufficient knowledge, you are asking for trouble. You should know many times more about the subject of your talk than you can possibly use. Your responsibility is to gather this material together in advance of your speaking effort.

Sources to Be Tapped for Knowledge

1. *Yourself.* The best source of knowledge is that which you have gathered from your environment, education, work, hobby, travel, etc. When you use something which you have personally experienced, you are the world's number one authority on such an item. There is no one who can challenge you on its accuracy. (Note how I used

personal knowledge in opening this chapter by relating my experience with the desk officer in Brooklyn.)

When Nikita Khruschev attended the United Nations Assembly in 1959, he was guest of honor at a banquet. He had a prepared speech, but he did not use it. Something which a previous speaker said made this Russian leader discard his speech and talk without notes for almost an hour. How could he do this? Because he had more knowledge concerning his subject than he could possibly use. His talk was related to communism, something which occupied almost every waking minute of his existence.

2. *Other people.* If you have little or no experience with the subject being researched, perhaps an acquaintance of yours has knowledge concerning it. Check with your friends and fellow workers. Ask your boss about it. If you have a sharp subordinate, discuss it with him (even if he can't help, he will respect you for having sought his counsel.) Find out who the experts are in such matters and get in touch with them. Contact anyone who might give you what you need.

3. *Literature.* After you have exhausted all leads for personal knowledge, go to the printed word. Visit the library and review the subject. As you read through newspapers and magazines, have a pair of scissors handy to cut out related items. Regarding these clippings, I urge you in the strongest possible terms to start your own background file. Before you actually need the material, anticipate what you may be required to talk about in the next five or ten years and start collecting items of interest.

In 1950, our professional study group gathered in the home of one of its members, Johannes Spreen. This ambitious young supervisor produced a cardboard box with a few dozen manila folders. This was the file he had started for the administrative subjects of planning, organizing, staffing, direction, coordinating, reporting, budgeting, public relations, equipment, and training. An orderly approach like this started John on the road to his present position of national prominence as an administrator in the field of criminal justice.

Many great speakers use this valuable research tool. They file clippings according to the titles of speeches they are going to give. Then, a few weeks before the talk, they review the collected items, select those to be used and thereby add to the knowledge needed for the talk.

4. *Other media.* As soon as you are scheduled to give a speech, you should extend your "knowledge gathering antenna" in all directions. If you are at the movies or the theatre, be on the alert for interesting items related to your subject. If you are watching television or listening to the radio, don't be completely passive. Have a pencil nearby and jot a note on a slip of paper for insertion into your "speech background file." Though this active listening or watching with a pad and pencil handy may sound like a nuisance, we predict that the opposite will be true. This new technique for deriving benefit will add a valuable dimension to your watching or listening pleasure.

Knowledge and the Guest Lecturer

Every year, an extraordinary series of meetings takes place in New York City. These meetings are designed to evaluate the qualifications of guest speakers who will make themselves available for paid appearances before audiences. Each of the speakers is an expert on a certain topic, bringing to the speaker's platform a lengthy association with his or her subject—often a lifetime of conscientious devotion. In the relatively short appearance before a civic, fraternal, business, or other type of group, the speaker must condense a wealth of background material into an interesting presentation. Although speaking techniques are important to success, the first and foremost credential is knowledge. The speaker with it stands a chance. The one lacking in knowledge won't even get by the auditions.

Knowledge and the Army

At one point in my career, I was considering a position on the faculty of the United States Military Academy at West Point. It was to be an assignment in the Leadership School teaching effective speaking. While acquainting myself with the curriculum, I came across the best speech on leadership I had ever read. It was delivered by a Major Bach to the graduating class at Fort Sheridan in 1917. He closed the speech with eight words that summarized leadership beautifully, "Know your men, know your job, know yourself."

Knowledge Is Indispensable

Just as being a leader depends on knowledge, so does your ability to hold an audience depend on knowledge. If you don't have it, don't attempt to deliver the speech. However, if you are now convinced that knowledge is indispensable to the success of a talk, let's proceed to the second *must*.

SINCERITY

It is not enough to know your subject, you must believe in it! Many men became famous because of their sincerity— because they believed wholeheartedly in the cause they were supporting.

In making this point, incidentally, we will use the names of dozens of individuals as examples to highlight specific points, some of whom will be associated with politics and religion. When citing these examples, our intent is not to attack, defend, or endorse any belief or ideology. Our only interest is to make a valid point in connection with effective speaking. Through the years, while lecturing on effective speaking, I have always made this declaration to avoid offending anyone, and to insure the highest possible degree of audience receptivity.

Sincerity and the Political Candidate

Some years ago, the former National Chairmen of the Republican and Democratic Parties (Len Hall and Jim Farley, respectively) were asked to identify the single most important ingredient in a presidential candidate's background. Both agreed that sincerity is the main thing in impressing the public.

Aldous Huxley in his book *Enemies of Freedom* goes a step further. He says, "All a successful campaign needs is a man who can be coached to *seem* sincere." Adlai Stevenson was asked about the validity of this statement and he said, "I'm afraid there is some truth to such a claim."

In the book, *The Selling of the President, 1968*,[1] the author contends that the Nixon the people saw during that campaign was the man the Nixon team wanted people to see. The image they wanted Nixon to project had many positive attributes, but, above all, he had to have sincerity.

When Hubert Humphrey was a boy in Minnesota, his father was a Republican. One night Mr. Humphrey

---

[1]Joe McGinniss, *The Selling of the President, 1968* (New York, Simon and Schuster, 1969).

went to hear a speech by an outstanding Democrat, William Jennings Bryan. Mr. Humphrey was so impressed by Bryan's sincerity that he switched political parties then and there.

Sincerity and Selling

Billy Graham has addressed more people, face to face, than any other man who ever lived. His ministry has taken him to the four corners of the earth. Do you know what this world-renowned preacher did in the first job of his career? He was a Fuller Brush salesman. After the first year, he was the top salesman in the Carolinas. He was asked for the secret of his success and he answered, "I believed in the product, and sincerity is the biggest part of selling anything."

Sincerity and Attitude

While I was discussing sincerity with a group of supervisors at the University of Buffalo, one of the listeners said it was difficult for a newly promoted supervisor to be sincere when he was lecturing to men who had been his work partners just a short time ago. He said he found it impossible to speak with conviction about strict adherence to work regulations when he had been lax on occasion while he was a member of the work group he was now supervising.

I replied by conceding that many supervisors were troubled by this apparent problem. However, the problem is not difficult to solve if a supervisor adopts the proper attitude. A worker gets paid to *do*, a supervisor gets paid to *supervise*. What a supervisor did when he was a worker should in no way affect the completely new scope of responsibilities he discharges as a supervisor. One passage from the Bible highlights how this transition should work. It says in essence, "When I was a child, I spoke as a child; now I am grown and I put away childish things." (1 Corinthians, Chapter 13, Verse 11) When a man grows to be a supervisor, he puts aside his activity as a worker. Adopt this attitude and there will be no problem in displaying sincerity as you carry out your new role as a leader.

Sincerity and Audience Response

It is a well-known fact that a teacher does not command the highest salary in the community. However, if he does his job well, he derives a sense of satisfaction that cannot be measured in dollars and cents. Sincerity is a speaking characteristic which promotes positive audience response and brings satisfaction to the speaker. At Fort Gordon, Georgia, I was conducting a Methods of Instruction Course. At the end of the first week I was approached by a student named Captain Pugh. He said that he had attended four years of college and never studied for an examination, yet he found himself at home during this M.O.I. course doing all kinds of preparation for his three-minute talk the next day. He wanted me to know that my constant sincerity had caused him to do what college hadn't. He couldn't let me down by not trying his best.

Similarly, when the Suffolk County Police Department was created, five of its high ranking officers attended my effective speaking course in New York City. They traveled sixty-five miles to get to class in the morning and sixty-five miles home in the evening. One of the five was extremely unhappy, and he took no pains to hide his displeasure during the first two days of the course. On the last day, each man had to give a short talk. When it came time for the annoyed executive to speak, I held my breath wondering what his parting remarks would be. A few minutes later I had a lump in my throat, my eyes were moist, and I felt like hugging Pat Mellon. Pat did a very courageous thing. In front of an audience, he apologized for his poor attitude at the beginning of the course. As he put it, he came to scorn but stayed to pray. He identified the single element that caused him to change his mind about the value of the course, that shifted his impressions from the negative to the positive. He said it was the instructor's sincerity, day after day.

Sincerity in a Controversial Figure

Throughout American history, there was never a more controversial figure than Senator Joseph McCarthy of Wisconsin. He was either admired or detested. His activities were so unique that new words had to be added to the dictionary to convey their true meaning. Many thought him to be a super-patriot while others regarded him as a ruthless character assassin.

Aware of these extremely divergent opinions of Senator McCarthy, I visited the Hotel Astor to hear him speak. He was extremely effective. At one point, he mentioned that he was a Captain in the United States Marines during World War II. His unit fought the Japanese in the Pacific. After an engagement with the enemy, he told how the personal effects of the young marines who had been killed in battle were brought to his tent. He related how he wrote to the mothers of these young men. He described how a hatred welled up in him against the forces of evil that had caused these deaths. Senator McCarthy pounded the rostrum as he related how Marine Captain McCarthy vowed to fight dictatorships with every ounce of his strength in the years to come. The audience exploded into applause and shouts of encouragement.

If ever a speaker sounded sincere it was Joe McCarthy. He believed in his principles although many, many people disagreed with them. To a large extent, this sincerity made him a power on the national scene.

Sincerity and Effective Teaching

Some years ago, *Time* magazine did a cover story on twelve of the "hottest" professors in colleges throughout the United States. It talked about each one, reported on his techniques and what made him a standout in his field. The most common attribute of these outstanding teachers was sincerity.

"You Gotta Believe!"

When the New York Mets won the 1973 pennant, they were sparked by a pitcher named Tug McGraw who kept repeating, "You gotta believe!" We hope we have convinced you that you "gotta believe" in your subject to deliver a top-notch speech.

ENTHUSIASM

It's not enough to know your subject and believe in it— you must be eager to talk about it!

In the past twenty-five years, I have listened to thousands of short talks given by people who were seeking to improve their speaking ability. Without a shadow of a doubt, the greatest single shortcoming in these two- or three-minute talks was a lack of enthusiasm. The great majority of these speakers knew their subject, they believed in it, but they didn't convey the impression that their message was important and that they were eager to tell the audience about it. They didn't let themselves go, didn't show true emotion, didn't get worked up; and as a result they didn't get a good response from the audience.

Enthusiasm and Emotion

For many years I observed and listened to Robert Wagner as he discharged his duties as Mayor of the City of New York. He never displayed emotion and I never responded affirmatively. Finally it came time for him to retire. On the front page of *The New York Times* was a picture of him giving his farewell speech and there were tears in his eyes. For the first time he showed me that he cared, and for the first time he earned an "A" for effective speaking.

Enthusiasm and Politics

Speaking of politics, the campaign for Governor of New York State in 1958 was a perfect example of the importance of enthusiasm. Averill Harriman was the incumbent and Nelson Rockefeller the challenger. Harriman had a big advantage in experience; he was a nationally prominent politician who had been present at the conferences after World War II in Russia with Stalin and Churchill. In addition, he was Governor. Rockefeller was relatively new to politics; the big thing he had going for him was the dubious distinction of being a part of the Rockefeller dynasty.

Looking at the contest from an effective speaking standpoint, we find that Harriman had the distinct advantage in knowledge. Because Harriman had such an outstanding record, we would have to give him the edge in sincerity as well. However, Rockefeller won the election because of his tremendous display of enthusiasm. He spoke Spanish to Puerto Ricans in Harlem, he ate bagels and lox with the Jewish population on the Lower East Side, he shook hands with voters in rolled-up shirtsleeves on the boardwalk at Coney Island. Everywhere he went and everytime he spoke, he was eager to meet his audience and expose them to his warm, affable personality. Harriman conducted an unenthusiastic campaign without getting excited and went down to a surprising defeat.

What Inhibits Enthusiasm?

Why is it that Harriman didn't display enthusiasm? Why is it that the great majority of people can't "let themselves go" in front of an audience? The reason lies deep within the average human being. To be reluctant to show emotion in front of others is a perfectly natural behavior pattern. To borrow from Freud, we could explain it in terms of the "id," the "ego," and the "super-ego."

The *id* is like the pure animal instinct. It is the desire to satisfy one's natural desires regardless of the circumstances. On a busy city street crowded with pedestrians a dog will obey its natural impulse to mate. Humans wouldn't do this because it is not approved by society. In his 1976 interview with *Playboy* magazine, President Carter indicated that he had lust in his mind toward a member of the opposite sex other than his wife. The average person, if he or she is honest and has natural impulses, would admit to the same emotion. What inhibits us from following our natural impulses? What holds the human in check? Let's consider the answer to these questions.

The Id and the Ego

An infant is controlled by the id. A baby wants its natural impulses to be satisfied *now*. If it feels the need to evacuate, it fills its diaper with absolutely no pangs of conscience. If it is hungry, it turns to the mother's breast; if the breast is not available, it cries because it is hungry and wants food *now*.

As the baby grows older, an adjustment develops between its id and reality. As a tiny infant, it lies on its back and stretches out its hand for a brightly colored rattle hanging from the top of the crib. The baby cannot possibly reach the rattle; unable to comprehend this fact, it keeps trying. Then one day the growing baby rolls over on its stomach, raises itself to its knees, grasps the side of the crib and pulls itself to the height where it can reach the rattle. The id now has a companion within the child called the "ego." The *ego* represents the adjustment of the natural impulse to the environment. The baby learns that it cannot satisfy all its needs unless it acts in a certain way.

The Superego

Our baby eventually grows into a child who can understand what is said by adults. At this stage begins the development of the effective speaking troublemaker, the factor that inhibits enthusiasm, the superego. The parents begin to make the child conform to their cultural standards with admonitions like, "Don't make noise . . . Don't mark the walls . . . Don't dirty your clothes . . . Don't, don't, don't!" By making the child aware of the curbs of society, the parents, the teachers and all the other controlling influences are sowing the seeds of adult inhibition. The *superego* is therefore said to be the conscience developed by society to keep the id in check.

Perhaps Shakespeare was thinking of this when he had Hamlet state that "conscience doth make cowards of us all." Have you ever watched small children at play? They are completely uninhibited and oblivious of the fact that anyone is watching. If they are playing cowboys and Indians or cops and robbers, they give performances that equal or surpass those of professionals for spontaneity and enthusiasm. Since the young child is such a natural performer, what is it that transforms him into an introverted grownup?

The youngster at home who becomes the student at school and who becomes a jobholder in the workaday world is required to conform to group standards for so long that it is difficult for him or her as an adult to stand all alone in front of a group and abruptly change longstanding behavior patterns. That is what we ask an adult to do when we encourage him to speak with enthusiasm.

Making the Transition from Inhibition to Enthusiasm

Because this transition is so difficult for the average adult, special techniques are sometimes employed to achieve the change. In a class situation, the group might be divided into two teams. As each member of a team tries to give a speech, the opposing team tries to shout him down. Of course the voices rise, gestures increase, laughter occurs, emotions become involved. Very often, for the first time in a speaker's adult career, he forgets his inhibitions and lets his natural impulses take over.

Another device is to let the speaker hold a folded cardboard or a rolled magazine. As he speaks, he is encouraged to pound the table or desk with the club. The physical act of swinging the club and the noise it makes serve to spur the speaker on to more and more enthusiasm.

Demosthenes did something like this when he went to the seashore and orated to the crashing waves. If, like Demosthenes, you choose to work by yourself, then use your imagination. Get your notes, close the doors and windows, step up to whatever you use for a lectern, imagine you are speaking to a thousand people—then shown them enthusiastically how eager you are to give them your message.

The Importance of Enthusiasm

F. W. Woolworth, when he was building his five-and-ten-cent store empire, surrounded himself with enthusiastic employees. He claimed that a second-rate worker with enthusiasm was more valuable than a first-rate worker without it.

Lincoln Steffens was enthusiastic about eliminating corruption in government. In his book[2] about the "muckraking" investigations of the early 1900s he mentioned several politicians he admired, one of whom was Senator Robert La Follette. The Senator was so excited about improving government that his speeches were exercises in calisthenics. On one occasion he battered his hand so badly by enthusiastically pounding it on the lectern that he had to carry it around in a sling for weeks.

Yousuf Karsh ranks among the greatest portrait photographers in the world. Over a thirty-five year period, his camera captured the images of the world's greatest men and women. From his studio in Ottawa, Canada, he would travel to Washington, London, Paris, or other

[2]The classic work, *The Muckrakers.*

cities to execute a portrait of some eminent world leader upon request. Why was a portrait by Karsh so great and so different? The answer won't be found in the use of a special studio, special lens, or special lighting equipment. The difference lay in Karsh himself. He explained, "I generate so much enthusiasm when working, that the subject becomes part and parcel of this enthusiasm." At the very instant that this enthusiasm is reflected by the subject, the shutter clicks and another portrait is added to the "gallery of greatness" by Karsh.

Enthusiasm Can Work Anywhere

To illustrate that enthusiasm doesn't require any special environment in which to take seed and grow, I recall its presence in the most unlikely of places. I participated in an effective speaking course at the Rikers Island Penitentiary. We instructors donated our time to this charitable program in the hope that some beneficial effects of the course would help the prisoner in making a successful adjustment when he returned to society at the termination of his sentence. It was heartening to see the way in which the inmates responded. Out there in that classroom in the middle of New York City's East River I heard more enthusiastic speeches than those given by some students in more academic surroundings.

An interesting sidelight to this course occurred one year after its conclusion. As field commander of New York City's Narcotic Bureau, I responded to the scene of every narcotics arrest in the city during my tour on duty. At the 28th Detective Squad in the heart of Harlem, I interviewed an addict who had been apprehended while in possession of a quantity of heroin. At the conclusion of my questioning the addict said, "I remember you from the effective speaking course on Rikers Island."

During our ensuing discussion he commented on how the course had helped him. He regretted that his heroin habit prevented him from putting his enthusiasm to work in the proper direction.

Enthusiasm and Selling

The Connecticut General Insurance Company understands the value of enthusiasm. It repeatedly runs full page ads in our most widely circulated magazines to preach the virtues of this highly prized personal characteristic. It uses catchlines like "Anchors hold ships, enthusiasm holds men." Sales managers and other supervisors whose success is measured by results, regard enthusiasm as the most important key to increased sales (when coupled with knowledge and sincerity, of course).

Note the construction of the word *enthusiasm*. If you break it down into syllables and alter the spelling slightly, "en-thus-i-asm" becomes "in-thus-I-am." In this form, it conveys the message that an individual is only as effective as the amount of enthusiasm he radiates. Very often when a man takes an effective speaking course, a sales course, or some other personality development course, his family and friends notice a change if the course helps him. They usually find that the graduate seems more alive. He smiles more often, greets more readily; in essence, he has become more enthusiastic.

Many personnel departments administer tests to evaluate the intelligence quotient of prospective employees. These I.Q. tests serve a purpose, but they are not the complete answer. They cannot measure that vital characteristic which a marketing giant like F. W. Woolworth put above all others—enthusiasm. This highly desirable trait can be measured only by personal observation, by seeing and hearing how the individual interacts in communication contacts with other human beings.

Enthusiasm and Acting

One evening I dropped into the Yiddish Theatre at 2nd Avenue and 2nd Street in Manhattan after the performance had begun. I remained in the rear watching Molly Picon, the stellar attraction of the Yiddish stage. The manager came over to me and whispered, "Would you believe it, she is over sixty years of age." It was hard to believe. Miss Picon had the bounce, the zest, the sparkle of a much younger woman. Again the manager whispered, "Every night before she comes on the stage, she does exercises." This fact is of significance to all who perform before audiences. Just as a professional baseball or basketball player would not begin a game without a warmup, so Molly Picon, at the top of her profession, wouldn't meet her audience until she was fully charged up. While those calisthenics served to loosen up her body, they also served to quicken her responses, to animate her expression, to increase her enthusiasm.

Enthusiasm and Preaching

The great preacher, Henry Ward Beecher, was once asked by a visiting minister, "Why is it that your audiences sit on the edge of their seats waiting for the next word while my congregation often goes to sleep during my sermon?" Reverend Beecher looked his fellow clergyman in the eye and said, "The remedy is simple. Get someone near the pulpit with a long stick. Have him watch the congregation closely. Every time a head begins to nod, the man should extend his stick and give *you* a prod in the backside." This is a radical method of generating more enthusiasm, but I'm sure speakers will get the point.

Increase Enthusiasm

Whether you employ Reverend Beecher's stick, Senator La Follette's pounding, Demosthenes' action at the shore, Molly Picon's exercises, F. W. Woolworth's personnel policies, or Yousuf Karsh's working technique to overcome your learned inhibitions is up to you. You should adopt the best device, the best formula, for you to increase your enthusiasm. If you concentrate on such a personality improvement, you will keep your super-ego under control and permit yourself to realize your potential as an effective speaker.

After adding "enthusiasm" to your "knowledge" and "sincerity," you can put them to work through the fourth *must* which we consider now.

PRACTICE

Effective speaking, in one respect, is no different from any other skill—practice makes perfect! If you want to excel at playing the piano, you play the piano. If you want to build up speed in typing, you type. If you have to run a mile race, you practice by running the mile. If you want to become a more effective speaker, you must speak before an audience! You can know your subject, believe in it, and be eager to tell about it; but unless you transform these factors into action, everything that has gone before will be wasted.

The Dollar Value of Practice

If you were to take a course in effective speaking, it would cost you hundreds of dollars more than the purchase price of this book. Would you be paying these hundreds of dollars for more content, or for different principles, or for better instruction? No, that large sum of money would be paid to give you the opportunity to *practice*. That is the main difference between this book and an effective speaking course. When you use this book you have to find an audience to give you practice; when you take a course, your fellow students serve as your audience at every class session. It may seem that hundreds of dollars is a lot to pay for the opportunity to practice, but if you are serious, it is worth it.

Practice and the Theatre

While I was in London, in 1958, Sir Laurence Olivier was appearing in *The Entertainer*. I walked up to the box office and asked for two tickets. The attendant laughed, then explained that the show was sold out three months before it opened. Olivier had refused a $250,000 offer to do a movie in order to star in this stage production for about $150 per week. Why did he choose to work so much harder for so much less money? The answer consists of one word, *practice*. Every so often the truly great actor must return to the stage. He must appear before an audience in order to practice and perfect all the acting skills that contribute to great performances.

Robert Preston explained the value of performing in the legitimate theatre by stating, "With live audiences, you get something when you give. They are always different; therefore I'm always different. I learn something at every performance."

Practice and Politics

President Kennedy tried to become the vice-presidential candidate in 1956 but he failed. He then set his sights on a presidential bid. During the next four years he talked to audiences throughout the United States. A newspaper article said, "There is no doubt that this is paying off in experience. Kennedy has always been effective in small gatherings. Now he is a much more effective platform speaker. He makes points with an assurance he did not have a few years ago." When one watched President Kennedy handle a news conference, it seemed as if the ability came to him naturally. Those who followed his career closely, know that his excellence before an audience came from long years of practice.

Practice and "Muscle Memory"

When a ballplayer, skilled dancer, or other performer practices, he repeats the same correct movement over and over. This repetition causes his body to react automatically when his brain calls for that movement. We call this *muscle memory*; doing the right thing without being conscious of each little movement. When an inexperienced speaker faces an audience, he doesn't know what to do with his hands, his eyes, or the rest of his body. The good speaker practices how to use his body. At first, he must make the movement consciously, but after a while muscle memory takes over and he finds himself able to concentrate on his notes while his hands, eyes, and body in general automatically do the right things.

Practice and Motion Pictures

When Frank Sinatra appeared in his first motion picture, his acting left a great deal to be desired. However, not too many years later he won an Academy Award for his performance in *From Here to Eternity.* Sinatra went from poor to excellent through practice.

Practice and Political Conventions

When Senator John Glenn of Ohio (and outer space) rose to make the keynote address at the 1976 Democratic Convention, he was about to make the most important political speech of his life. If the speech was outstanding, he would probably be nominated for vice-president. If the speech failed, he would not be so nominated. The speech failed.

As I watched Senator Glenn trying unsuccessfully to capture the full attention of the restless, preoccupied mass of delegates, I was reminded of a similar scene at the Republican Convention back in 1952. Senator Everett Dirksen was on the platform before an unruly mass of delegates. The opposing slate was making a surge and Dirksen wanted to stop it. He stood on the platform minute after minute after minute, respectfully asking for attention. Slowly the noise subsided. Dirksen waited and waited and asked for silence. Finally he had silence and he delivered a great speech. Senator Dirksen was a master speech-maker. Only a true expert could control a crowd of that type. Dirksen had long years of practice; Glenn did not. That made a big difference.

Why You Should Practice

In the chapters to come we will discuss *what* you should practice, *when* you should practice, *where* you should practice, and *how* you should practice. At this point we are concerned only with the answer to the question of *why* you should practice and *why* you should accept every opportunity to speak.

The obvious answer is to improve. However, there is a psychological factor involved. If you have a negative attitude toward practice and you don't seek every opportunity to speak, then each speech situation you face will be fraught with indecision and anxiety. On the other hand, if you make a resolution that from now until your speaking career ends you will accept every possible opportunity to speak, you will have taken a long step forward. Indecision and anxiety will be replaced by confidence and poise. Of course it will mean work, but each time you prepare and rehearse a speech you will improve your ability.

Shakespeare's Julius Caesar put it well when he said, "The coward dies a thousand deaths, the valiant never taste of death but once." Let the cowards die each time a speech situation comes before them. Be valiant—resolve once and for all to accept every invitation to speak.

THE IMPORTANCE OF THE "MUSTS"

If, after you have completed this book, you remember only what you have read about the *musts,* you will have derived a great deal of benefit. To do justice to any speech situation, you must have knowledge, sincerity, enthusiasm, and practice. What lies ahead in this text will refine your speaking ability, will enrich your speech content, and will heighten the enjoyment and satisfaction to be derived from one of the most stimulating experiences on earth, that of speaking to an audience.

two
The
"Don't Worries"
of Effective
Speaking

Aspiring speakers often conjure up problems even when there isn't a cloud on the horizon. They imagine great difficulties, when, in reality, they are their own worst enemies for taking a negative view. Over the years I have had many students come to me in confidence and say, "This effective speaking is great for the average person, but, unfortunately, it is no good for me. You see, I . . ." They then finish the sentence by mentioning something unimportant, something in the "Don't Worry" category. Many factors are *mistakenly* regarded as insurmountable barriers to a successful speaking career. We will show how some of these supposed barriers can be scaled, how others can be avoided, and how others can be made to disappear.

One factor in particular, erroneously thought of as an emotional barrier, can be turned almost magically into a most valuable asset. Let us begin with this misunderstood factor, which is unwittingly regarded by the

unsophisticated as harmful. In reality, this emotion—
nervousness—is an invaluable aid to the enlightened performer.

DON'T WORRY ABOUT NERVOUSNESS

If you were in my effective speaking course, I would not
announce in advance that I was going to discuss nervousness. Instead, I would get everybody in the class into a
state of nervousness so they would know what we were
talking about.

Here is how it would be done. First, I make this
statement to the class: "Near the end of our discussion
of the *musts,* we recommended that you make a resolution
to accept all speaking invitations. At this time, we are
going to call upon one individual in this class to give a
short talk. It will be for only three minutes and you can
talk on any subject. We will select the speaker at random.
I will pick a number, say forty-two and begin to count as
I point to members of the class. Whomever I point to
when I say 'forty-two' will be our speaker. Let us begin
the counting: one, two, three. . . ."

As the count slowly progresses, the tension in the
room mounts. When I get to number thirty-eight, I stop
counting and pause. I say to the class, "Please note your
physical condition at this moment to see whether you
have any of the following symptoms: pounding at the
temples, dry mouth, wet underarms, lump in throat, faster
heartbeat, butterflies in stomach or bottom dropped out
of stomach, perspiring hands or weak knees. I hope that
all of you experienced at least one of these symptoms.
Why? Because they are signs of nervousness. If you

didn't undergo any physical change, then one of two things affects your particular case. Either you are too stupid to enjoy the sensation of nervousness or you don't care about doing a good job. But, if you have normal intelligence and you want to do a good job, you *must* be nervous."

I began using this technique in 1954. In more than twenty years, I never had a student object to being called "stupid" or being accused of "not caring." This history is a pretty good indication that the wonderful symptoms of nervousness were generously distributed throughout all those audiences.

I especially emphasized the value of nervousness in my Methods of Instruction courses. After exposing the newly assigned instructors to the "nervousness generating countdown device," I gave them a word of advice. I advised them to request a transfer from instructional duties if they hadn't become nervous. This counsel was based on the assumption that they were not stupid, and therefore a lack of nervousness indicated a lack of concern about doing a good job.

The External Causes of Nervousness

We have described nervousness as "most valuable" and "wonderful." We could accord it other glowing adjectives and not be guilty of gilding the lily. Nervousness is wonderful because it is nature's way of preparing the body to meet an emergency. It is nature's way of sensitizing each one of our senses so that we can respond faster, perform better, and concentrate more intensely.

We become nervous when we are faced with a challenge, when we have cause to be concerned, or, to be frank, when we are afraid. Fear is a very normal emotion, occuring when any of our five senses comes into contact with danger. Your sense of smell may detect the odor of something burning in your home at 3AM. Your sense of touch may tell you that your front door is open when you know you locked it a few hours ago. Your sense of sight may make you aware of the audience you are about to face. Your sense of hearing may signal your brain that you have just been introduced as the next speaker. Any of these situations would be cause for nervousness because one of your senses prompted you to have fear.

Physiological Reasons for Nervousness

We have considered the *external* causes of nervousness. Now let us examine what goes on *inside* the body—what physiological changes accompany nervousness and make us capable of better performance.

When any of our senses perceives a fearful situation, it instantaneously sends a message of alarm to the brain. All in the same instant, the brain relays the message to the adrenal gland, which releases adrenalin into the blood. The blood stream surges the adrenalin to the heart which, thus stimulated, pumps faster, causing an instantaneous increase in the pulse rate and consequently in the supply of blood to all the vital organs—including our senses. In the time it takes to blink your eyes, you can now see, hear, taste, feel, smell, and think better. This miracle of instantaneous response occurs in all normal persons and offers tremendous benefit to those who accept it and make it work for them.

In 1964, the United States Office of Education awarded $5,000 to the University of Illinois to find a cure for stage fright. At that time I suggested to my classes that the effort would be unsuccessful. To date, no cure has been announced and I can assure you that it is not forthcoming. To be nervous is as natural as breathing. To change it would be harmful, to eliminate it would be disastrous.

Let's Look at the Record

You may feel that our explanation of the cause and effect of nervousness is oversimplified. You may doubt that everybody experiences it, and you may question the fact that many enlightened individuals profit by its presence. You may want proof. If this is the case, let's look at the record!

Helen Hayes is one of the most respected names in the history of the American stage. So highly regarded is she that a Broadway theatre was named in her honor. On the occasion of the opening of that theatre, she was interviewed by a reporter. He asked her if, after her long stage career, she *ever* became nervous before a performance. She answered, "On the day after the night when I fail to become nervous, that is the day on which I will retire from the stage." In other words, Helen Hayes, after thousands of performances, still became nervous before each new audience.

Anyone who witnessed a performance by the debonair Frenchman, Maurice Chevalier, would find it hard to believe that, at one time, he didn't know how to utilize nervousness. As a very young man singing before an audience he became nervous, forgot a line, panicked, and had to leave the stage. It happened a second time and he left Paris to think about a new career. In the small town of Saujon he met a Dr. Dubois who listened to his problem. The doctor said, "Maurice, don't be afraid to be afraid." Chavalier accepted the advice, went back to Paris, and found success. Thereafter, for more than forty years, he accepted fear as a normal thing and he used the nervousness it produced to help him achieve a most illustrious career.

Chuck McKinley, a former U.S. Open Tennis Champion, once said, "If I'm not nervous, I lose." In other words he had to be nervous to play his best.

The great baseball star, Stan Musial, once said, "At the end of every game I'm beat because of the strain on the nervous system." It wasn't the running or hitting or throwing that wore him out, it was the effect of nervousness which built up and couldn't be expended. An outfielder in a baseball game may get two or three fly balls in a whole game, yet he is on edge with every one of the pitches thrown to the batter. That's why you will see so many ball players pounding their glove, tugging at their cap, kicking at the dirt, or doing something else to work off their nervousness.

Byron Nelson, the great golfer, said that he became ill and threw up before some tournaments. Here again we see an accumulation of nervousness in evidence. Nelson was nervous before the tournament and it caused him distress because he had no adequate way to work it off. Once the tournament started, there was no problem, he used up nervousness to play better.

When Doug Ford won the Masters at Augusta he shot a blistering 66 on the last day. Someone remarked that Ford must have no nerves. I knew this to be untrue because I saw a light sweater which Doug wore become soaking wet from nervous perspiration from the armpit down to the elbow.

Golfer Jimmy Demaret asked the great Arnold Palmer what he did when he needed a birdie and a par on the last two holes to win a tournament. Palmer said, "I get nervous, and the adrenalin starts to flow."

John Newcombe, the Australian tennis star, also

referred to the help he received from his flow of adrenalin during a tough match in the U.S. Open at Forest Hills.

In the theatre, here is a list of some performers who become nervous. Paul Muni got sick to his stomach on the opening night of *Inherit the Wind* as he approached the theatre and saw his name in lights. Jimmy Stewart has never been able to overcome the "fear thing" during the anticipation part of acting. Robert Taylor was as nervous at the end of his thirty-year career as he was at the beginning. Jimmy Durante always went on the stage nervous. Bobby Darin didn't shake nervousness until after his first song; Elvis Presley was the same. Milton Berle feels himself fortunate for being nervous. Jerry Lewis, Phil Silvers, Nancy Walker, and Jackie Gleason all take a few minutes to settle down after the curtain has gone up. Richard Burton can't sleep the night before a show opens. Four days before *Hello Dolly* opened, Carol Channing lost her appetite. Gertrude Lawrence claimed that her pre-performance anxieties increased as the years went by. When Cornelia Otis Skinner asked her father how long it would take to overcome her anxieties he answered, "All your life." Alfred Lunt felt tense before every performance over a fifty-year career; Lynn Fontanne said that any performer who claimed he wasn't frightened just wasn't telling the truth. Another great team, Anne Jackson and Eli Wallach admit to the shakes. Alec Guinness is affected several days before a new show opens. Bert Lahr had the jitters throughout his long career as a comedian. Jose Ferrer would rest before performances to calm his nerves.

Telford Taylor, Chief Counsel at the Nuremberg War Crimes trials and noted author, stated that, "Adolf Hitler was certainly the most remarkable platform orator of modern times. Great crowds stimulated and sensitized

Hitler." This is another way of saying that a large audience made Hitler nervous and more effective.

Ben Hogan is regarded by golfers as one of that game's all-time greats. He once remarked, "If you don't get nervous you are not human." Arthur Ashe, former U.S. Open and Wimbledon champion, says that everybody "chokes" at one time or another. Arthur claims that the best way to avoid it is sound concentration on the positive elements of trying to win.

After Cardinal Spellman's death, his staff remembered him as being nervous at big ceremonies. Former President Ford admitted that he got butterflies before an important speech.

What the Record of Nervousness Means

The record speaks for itself. In practically every activity where a performer is scheduled to appear before an audience, it has been proven that there is fear, choking, stage-fright, jitters, tension, anxiety, loss of appetite, sleeplessness, sickness, and a few other side-effects of nervousness. But, the important thing is that the artists with these assorted maladies suffer them because they care, because they want to do the best job possible. Many have said that they welcome these signs of nervousness because they know its presence will help them to be in top form.

Conversely, when these signs of nervousness subside or disappear, the stars are in trouble. When this happens you will hear statements like that of basketball's Bob Cousy: "I have to look for methods to get myself worked up for ball games to overcome a feeling of complacency." Or of tennis' Billie Jean King: "I can't seem to get intense. I need to be more emotional, to have some driving motivation." Or of golfer Bert Yancey: "I lost the Masters at Augusta on the last three holes. I thought I was getting psyched up, instead I went blank." These three great players are bewailing the fact that nervousness was absent, and they failed to get that extra lift they needed.

Make Nervousness Work for You

Can you imagine the nervousness of an astronaut sitting in a space-craft waiting to be propelled toward a target like the moon? Colonel John Glenn thought deeply about this and his observations are significant. He regards fear as perfectly normal. If it paralyzes, it is harmful. If it is controlled, it can be beneficial. He feels that the best thing we can do to control fear is to know all we can about a situation.

This principle can well be applied to effective speaking. You are now well-informed about the psychological and physiological aspects of nervousness. You know it is good, you know it is necessary. In the future, when you feel nervous, don't be a rank amateur and become flustered and ineffective. Instead, be a professional: Accept the wonderful sensation of nervousness and let it help you to give a better performance.

DON'T WORRY ABOUT SHYNESS

Shyness is also a perfectly natural sensation. It is felt in varying degrees by all human beings during some phase of their lives. Some people are shy about doing almost anything in public. Some people are shy because of their appearance. Some are shy because of lack of education. Some are shy when they are young but grow out of it. Some are not shy when they are young but become shy as they grow older. In other words, although shyness is universal, it manifests itself in a unique way in each individual.

In some people, a little shyness is a decided asset. It is a delight to encounter a beautiful girl, who at age 18, is still a trifle shy upon meeting a handsome young man. Conversely, it is almost tragic to find a talented, attractive person who is shy to the point of being incapable of profitably engaging in normal, everyday activities with other human beings.

There is no question that shyness is related to fear. This means nervousness is closely related to shyness. The fear that triggers nervousness operates in the same way as the fear that triggers shyness. For example, if a young man is shy in the presence of females, he will become afraid when one of his senses detects a female nearby. A danger signal is sent to his brain when his eyes see a girl approaching, or his ears hear that girl, or his nose smells her perfume, or any part of his body touches any part of that girl's body. As in nervousness, the boy's vital organs then react similarly to the fear syndrome.

In the play, *She Stoops to Conquer*, the hero approaches the heroine in two different ways. When he mistook her for a maid, he was forward, assertive, and assured. When she was present in her true role as a lady, he was shy and backward.

Such a change of personality under different conditions is not unusual in real life. In our section headed "The Help of Being Confident," you will find that Sir Alec Guinness and other persons exhibit such dual personalities. It is not at all unusual for the platform manner of an effective speaker to differ greatly from his normal life style.

A Personal Note

I dislike cocktail parties. They make me ill at ease. It is difficult for me to converse with different people about different things. Based on this, one might assume that I would be doubly uncomfortable in front of a large group because I don't handle myself well with cocktail conversation. Yet, *the opposite is true.* Large audiences stimulate me to perform well, and I enjoy doing so.

If you are shy about speaking, don't worry about it. You have a lot of company because everyone is shy about something. What should you do? Read and reread the sections on nervousness and being confident. Concentrate on sincerity and enthusiasm. One day you will burst out of your cocoon of shyness and become an effective speaker. I have seen it happen many times, and it will happen to you if you care enough to persevere.

DON'T WORRY ABOUT "ER'S" AND "AH'S"

When we suggest not to worry about "er's" and "ah's," we are not implying that they are desirable. They serve no good purpose. However, the usual case of "er's" and "ah's" is not so serious that you should get upset about it. In an extreme case, these useless sounds may be long, drawn out, and frequent.

In such a situation, corrective steps have to be taken. The simplest way of correcting the problem is to close your mouth between statements! It is impossible to say "er" or "ah" when the lips are sealed. For the average case of "er's" and "ah's," some intelligent practice will alleviate the condition. In a later chapter we will discuss the highly beneficial impact of pauses. If a speaker merely substitutes pauses for "er's" and "ah's," he reaps a twofold dividend: he eliminates a fault and he gains an asset.

Ask Someone to Check Your Speech

Few people are aware that they use "er's" and "ah's" when they speak in public. The only way they will be made cognizant of their fault is if someone tells them. Whenever you speak to an audience, therefore, try to have a friend present to evaluate your effort. Ask your critic not to pull any punches but to tell it like it is about all your faults.

Your spouse will give criticism readily, so he or she might be a good evaluator. For example, when George Romney was seeking the presidential nomination, it became known that his wife was an outstanding speaker. When she listened to Romney speak, her approval or disapproval was vividly reflected by her facial expression. Newspaper reporters began to watch her reactions until she became aware of what was happening. She then adopted a deadpan face and kept her true feelings for Romney's ears alone.

DON'T WORRY ABOUT YOUR VOICE

There is no question that a speaker's effectiveness is increased if he has a voice like a radio announcer. But is it necessary? It is no more necessary than it is for a girl to have a beautiful face and a perfect figure in order to impress an audience.

You may think that an above-average voice is a basic requirement for an effective speaker. This is not so. If you have an average voice you will start with an advantage over many great men who made outstanding speeches. Abraham Lincoln had a poor voice yet he acquired great success through his speaking ability. Theodore Roosevelt's voice didn't sound pleasant yet his sincerity and enthusiasm made his listeners forget all about his vocal equipment.

There is ample evidence to show that a speaker with

an average voice can lecture for an extended period of time with little or no difficulty. From 1953 to 1958 I trained and supervised a staff of sixty instructors. These men were required to teach for three hours in the morning or afternoon. In those five years, we never encountered an instructor whose voice was unable to function satisfactorily.

There may be special requirements calling for certain voice characteristics which you do not have and must be developed. For example, when I attended Officer Candidate School, it was necessary to project one's voice on the parade grounds so that it would carry for great distances. Those of us who did not have strong voices would go out to the parade grounds in the evening and shout back and forth until we had built our volume up to an acceptable level.

Dr. Locke, Director of Psychology at a Veterans Hospital, described a patient who could not speak normally because of an operation. He had to learn to speak through a hole in his throat. In spite of this, he became an effective speaker. This extreme example should convince us that there isn't much point in worrying about an average voice.

DON'T WORRY ABOUT AN ACCENT

If President Carter had worried about his accent, he would never have stopped growing peanuts back in Georgia. Instead of worrying, Jimmy Carter couldn't wait to give his message to the voting population of the United States and his southern drawl didn't destroy the effectiveness of his delivery. Jimmy Carter was knowledgeable, sincere, enthusiastic, and he practiced good speech techniques across the length and breadth of America.

If you have an accent, don't worry about it if your audience can understand what you are saying. For many speakers, as in the case of comedian Victor Borge, a slight accent adds to effectiveness. However, if your accent is so strong that it prevents understanding, then you must improve your pronunciation to an acceptable degree before you attempt to deliver a speech to an English-speaking audience.

DON'T WORRY ABOUT VOCABULARY

There is no accomplishment in the field of education to be prized more highly than the development of an extensive vocabulary, you should not worry about your vocabulary dicator of how successful a man will become is the size of his vocabulary. It is a tremendous asset for a speaker to have a broad grasp of the English language and to use it skillfully. In spite of all these glowing statements about vocabulary, you should not worry about your vocabulary if it is only average or below-average.

Let's face it. You bought this book because you want to become a more effective speaker, and you can do so without an extensive vocabulary. We bring up the subject only to prevent you from becoming discouraged. Those of us who are not richly endowed in certain areas are sometimes afflicted with gnawing doubts. We doubt whether we can achieve a certain goal because we lack the background. If this doubt is not dissipated, it grows out of proportion and the quest for the goal is abandoned. Rest assured, although you have only a limited vocabulary, you can be a very effective speaker if you have the *musts*.

Lincoln's *Gettysburg Address,* for example, is an absolute classic, yet it is written in the simplest language. Examine it and see if you can find a word a high school student couldn't understand.

While you are becoming an effective speaker, however, you can do something about enlarging your vocabulary. There are many worthwhile pocketbooks on this subject.

During your effective speaking career, you should adjust your vocabulary to your audience. If you are talking to children, your vocabulary should be set at an elementary level. If you are addressing adults, it would be at a higher level. If you are lecturing to a professional group on a technical subject, you would employ the vocabulary and terminology appropriate to the occasion.

Later in this book we will discuss semantics, philology, and other areas related to vocabulary.

DON'T WORRY ABOUT EDUCATION

In 1920, shortly after he arrived from his native Ireland, Edward Heslin was a guard at New York's Metropolitan Museum of Art. He was posted at the Cellini Collection. He was extremely interested in the masterpieces for which he was responsible. Each day there would be a guided tour and each day the expert on Cellini would give his lecture by Heslin's post. Ed would listen intently and after the group left he would inspect the collection with increased interest. One day the regular lecturer was sick and the scheduled group entered the room and wandered about aimlessly. Ed couldn't bear to see them leave without hearing about the collection so he said, "Ladies and gentlemen, please step this way." Ed proceeded to deliver a lecture on Cellini. The following week he was called into the head curator's office. He was asked, "Mr. Heslin, did you lecture to a group last week?" Heslin said he had, whereupon he was directed never to do it again. The curator then gave Ed his congratulations. The Museum had received a letter from a woman in Canada who extended her compliments. She said she had never heard a better lecture on Cellini in her life than that given by Mr. Heslin. Ed Heslin never graduated from elementary school yet he was able to address a cultured audience in a manner that elicited praise.

The Shortstop and the Professor

In one of my classes, there were two students whose background and performance differed greatly. One was a shortstop in the minor leagues; the other was a college professor. Week after week the students received a speech assignment, and week after week they delivered their speeches. Week after week, the shortstop's speeches were terrific. Week after week, the professor's speeches were a bore. Although the shortstop had little educational background, he had knowledge, sincerity, enthusiasm, and he couldn't wait to get up there on the platform to practice. The professor was so concerned with using large words and maintaining his pedagogical decorum that the class never responded warmly. One evening, an angry professor surprised everyone by forgetting his educational background and speaking with enthusiasm and sincerity. On the way to our class, he was accosted by a sex pervert. The professor was so disturbed by the incident that he discarded the speech he had prepared and talked about the decline in public morals instead. The speech was great, the applause was loud, and the professor learned a valuable lesson in effective speaking.

College Degrees and Speaking Ability

During the early years of my speaking career, I did not have a college degree. However, I had the four *musts*, which provided me with a fair amount of success as a lecturer. After obtaining my first degree, my effectiveness did not automatically improve; it stayed about the same. My second degree was awarded summa cum laude and I was chosen class valedictorian. Again, no magical increase in my ability to impress an audience.

On an earlier page, I mentioned that I was responsible for the supervision of approximately sixty instructors for several years. Half these men were college graduates, half were not. Surprisingly, the number of instructors who earned the rating of "excellent" or "superior" was far higher in the non-college group than in the college group. How come? One would expect the reverse to be true.

After weighing all the factors over a considerable period, I came to the conclusion that it was a case of sincerity and enthusiasm. These two desirable characteristics proved to be more important to teaching excellence than a college degree. It was found that every single non-college instructor had *applied* for the assignment—presumably because he liked or loved to teach. He was sincerely interested in his students, and he was enthusiastic in the classroom. On the other hand, almost every college graduate was extended an *invitation* to join the teaching staff because of his educational background. Some accepted the invitation because they liked or loved to teach, but many agreed to enter the teaching field solely because the working conditions were more pleasant than the job they were holding when asked. These college men had less sincerity, less enthusiasm, and less effectiveness.

Lest I be accused of harboring a prejudice against

educated people, let me make one thing clear. Assume that I had to select sixty instructors from the information contained in employment questionnaires submitted by 120 men without being able to observe them teaching or without being able to interview them. Assume further that sixty of these men were college graduates and sixty had not attended college. All other things being equal, I would unhesitatingly select the sixty men who had graduated from college.

Although a college degree does not, *ipso facto,* make one a better speaker, it unquestionably provides him or her with many clear advantages which only formal education can give. As in the case of vocabulary, if you do not now have a good education, don't worry about it. However, in the future, if the opportunity presents itself, go back to school. If you can't find the time or money to pursue a college degree, take pertinent courses that will further your career. I wholeheartedly endorse courses offered by Dale Carnegie Associates and the American Management Association. Having been active with some of these courses in New York, New Jersey, and Georgia, I can say without reservation that great benefits accrue to the student who applies their principles.

DON'T WORRY ABOUT
AUDIENCE OPINION

During a five-year period in my teaching career, I wrote, produced, directed, and performed in stage productions. I know how it feels to stand behind the curtain, waiting for it to open, knowing that there are more than a thousand people out there in the orchestra, boxes, and balcony waiting to pass judgment on your performance. You can stand there worrying about it and accomplish nothing or, like Molly Picon with her exercises, you can do something constructive that will make you more effective when you face the audience. One famous opera star in this situation would stand behind the curtain whispering, "I love you, I love you, I love you" in the direction of the audience. This positive attitude was reflected in her face, body, and voice when the curtains parted, and she made the all-important initial contact with the audience.

President Kennedy's Technique

When Senator John Kennedy was preparing for a presidential bid in 1960, he visited state after state to obtain support. He realized that some of these states had helped to defeat him when he tried for the vice-presidency in 1956. Did he worry about audience opinion when he addressed Democratic Party gatherings in these states? The answer lies in the manner in which Jack Kennedy opened these talks. He began, "Thank you very much for voting against me in 1956. If I had run for vice-president at that time, my chance for the presidency at this time would not exist." Good-natured laughter would follow, then would come the serious appeal which laid the foundation for the making of President Kennedy.

Mark Antony's Technique

A classic example of not worrying about audience opinion, while trying to change it, is provided by Shakespeare's Mark Antony orating after the death of his friend Julius Caesar. He knew that the Roman citizenry were generally sympathetic to Brutus and the conspirators and antagonistic toward the supporters of the dead Caesar. So what did Mark Antony do? He accented the positive; he made statements at the outset with which the audience

would not take issue. He said, "Friends, Romans, countrymen, lend me your ears" (audience response: Okay, but
only a loan). "I come to bury Caesar not to praise him"
(audience response: as long as you don't say nice things).
"The evil that men do live after them; the good is often
interred with their bones; so let it be with Caesar" (audience
response: okay, so let it be.)

Mark Antony continued to make positive remarks
to include Brutus, then he evidenced slight sarcasm
about Brutus, eventually becoming critical of the conspirators who had slain Caesar. At the close of his talk,
the audience opinion had been changed completely and
they were now seeking revenge for their Caesar's murder.

A South Bronx Block Party

In 1942, shortly after the United States entered World
War II, there was fear that the East Coast would be
attacked. In New York City, there was a vigorous campaign to enlist air raid wardens. I was assigned to the
recruitment effort in the South Bronx. Each evening, a
designated block was closed off at each end. At eight
o'clock, patriotic music was played to attract a crowd.
Fifteen minutes later, I was introduced. I mounted the
platform and described the bombing and burning of
London; I warned the residents of the block that it could
happen in their neighborhood; and then I made a fervent
appeal for volunteers.

Was this type of recruitment campaign successful?
Only to a limited degree. We got a lot more abuse than
applications—this was a tough neighborhood. While I
was speaking, there were such cries as "How come you
don't volunteer for the Army?" If I had worried about
audience opinion as I rose to speak, I couldn't have

uttered an intelligible sentence. However, I believed wholeheartedly that our program was needed (sincerity), and I couldn't wait to try to convince those tough Irishmen to cooperate (enthusiasm).

President Johnson's Technique

When the New York World's Fair opened in 1964, President Johnson made the opening address with difficulty. The words "with difficulty" were added because, as the President started his talk, a group of pickets began to chant loudly. The chanting continued during the entire five minutes it took to complete the speech. None of the newsmen present could recall when a President had been shown such discourtesy. How did President Johnson react? Jack Gould of *The New York Times* wrote, "Mr. Johnson's demeanor was something that had to be seen. He understandably looked uncomfortable, but not a flicker of overt disapproval could be discerned on his face. Not a significant break in the rhythm of his words occurred." Although listeners winced at the subjection of the President to such bad manners and disrespect, the President transcended rudeness by not worrying about the opinion of one segment of his audience.

A Silent Opening Statement

For fifteen years I lectured on effective speaking as a consultant for the State of New York. My travels took me to every part of the state. Each time I faced a new audience, I stood before them without saying a word. I then picked up a sign, displayed it, and waited until everyone had read:

> THE AUDIENCE HAS
>
> FORMED AN OPINION

Then in silence I would flip the sign to reveal the words:

> AND NOT A WORD
>
> HAS BEEN SPOKEN

I then gave reasons why people form opinions, cited the importance of reinforcing favorable opinions, and emphasized the necessity of changing unfavorable opinions.

Don't Become Frustrated by Audience Opinion

The Christian and Jewish religions have been preaching their gospels for about two thousand and five thousand years respectively. They do not get complete cooperation but they never stop trying. In your effective speaking career, you will not be successful on every occasion. Don't become frustrated. Concentrate more on the *musts*, and audience opinion will be more favorable.

DON'T WORRY ABOUT BREATHING FROM THE DIAPHRAGM

Breathing from the diaphragm is the preferred way for speakers to utilize their breathing apparatus. However, unless you have breathing difficulties, you should not worry about this aspect of effective speaking.

Before we discuss the ideal way for speakers to breathe, let's review the way in which your breathing apparatus should operate when you breathe normally. When you inhale, your stomach area should be distended, should go outward. When you exhale, your stomach area should be drawn in.

Opera singers who rely on superb breath control must concentrate on breathing from the diaphragm. Some actors and speakers, whose artistry demands the highest level of achievement in every facet of their performance, also concentrate on breathing from the diaphragm. If you would like to experience how it feels to speak with the diaphragm in the ideal position, do the following: start to yawn, stop, hold your diaphragm in that position, and begin to speak.

DON'T WORRY ABOUT YOUR
SPEAKING FAULTS

Some years ago, Billy Graham conducted a three-day crusade in Madison Square Garden. The average person would have worried about what appeared to be a serious fault; the speaker was unable to speak the language of his audience! This fact did not concern Reverend Graham in the least. Although he could not speak the Spanish of the Puerto Rican audiences, Dr. Graham spoke through an interpreter. "Most observers," said a reporter, "were amazed that Billy Graham's appeal could be so dramatically transmitted through the use of an interpreter."

Faults won't kill a speech but lack of *musts* will. If you have knowledge, sincerity, enthusiasm, and you practice, you are going to be a success regardless of your faults.

A Speaker Who Didn't Worry About Blindness

Shortly before his death. Dale Carnegie presided at a commencement exercise where a speech competition was the highlight of the evening. There were five of us competing, but four, including me, never had a chance. The girl who won had to be led to and from the speaker's lectern because she was completely blind. In spite of this drawback, she performed magnificently. Instead of arousing pity, her speaking effort evoked admiration. After the voice, the eyes are the most valuable speaking tool a speaker possesses. This fact didn't phase this young lady in the least. She had no time to worry about her speaking handicap, she was too busy doing a tremendous job.

A Student Who Misjudged Speaking Ability

Whenever I conduct an effective speaking course, it always includes short talks given by each student. During such a talk a student once exclaimed, "Effective speaking is for the birds." He went on to explain that his boss was a rough-and-tumble guy who made a tremendous impression on his men and the public even though he couldn't speak effectively. After he sat down, I requested his permission to ask a few questions. "Shoot," said the student. "Does your boss know his job?" I asked. "Backwards and forwards," answered the student. "Does your boss believe in his work?" "He'll fight you if you say anything bad about it." "Is your boss interested in doing a good job?" "And how! He never seems to want to go home." "Does your boss ever talk to groups?" "Sure. He talks to the men and to civic organizations, but he's not an effective speaker." "Sir," I said, "your boss sounds like an effective speaker. Your answers tell us that he has knowledge, sincerity, enthusiasm and that he practices." This student mistakenly thought that a "rough-and-tumble guy" had speaking faults which prevented him from being effective. Not so.

A Texan Who Worried Needlessly

During the Vietnam War, I represented Fort Gordon in a tennis tournament at Fort Benning, Georgia. My doubles partner was a Texan named Garland Wade. After becoming better acquainted, he learned of my love for effective speaking. He then said something which amazed me. In all seriousness he declared, "I can never be an effective speaker because I have a sibilant *s* deficiency in my speech." After getting over my shock, I asked him about this ridiculous conclusion. He said that his high school teacher had told him, that although he was an excellent grammar student, he was the worst speaker she had ever met because of his sibilant *s*. He believed her and he was convinced that his supposed speaking fault was a permanent bar to his ever speaking effectively. I told Garland that her evaluation of his ability was absolute rubbish. "In fact," I added, "only three days ago I complimented your manner of speaking to Captain Johnson of the Civil Affairs School."

Don't Ignore Faults

Although we suggest that you not worry about speaking faults, you should, if they come to your attention, try to correct them. You may discover them yourself but self-discovery is rare. More often, someone will tell you about them. Again we recommend that you have a critic in the audience who will provide a feedback on your effectiveness or ineffectiveness.

A Good Way to Cure Faults

The next chapter deals with *helps*. It is very likely that its pages will contain a remedy for some fault that is troubling you. One thing is very likely: if you concentrate on using the *helps* properly, then, without your knowing it, your faults may disappear. They may disappear, not because you applied specific measures to correct them but because they were replaced by desirable speech characteristics.

three

The "Helps" Relating to Speech Organization

The *musts* of effective speaking are essential. However, unless we organize our speech properly, much of the knowledge, sincerity, enthusiasm, and practice will go to waste. In this chapter we will present guidelines to construct a speech that will permit the *musts* to realize their full potential.

THE "HELP" OF GOOD PREPARATION

If you approach the task of preparation in a workman-like manner, it will pay rich dividends in the savings of time and the production of an acceptable speech. We will consider five steps in the preparation process.

How to Prepare (The Five-Step Method)

1. *Estimate the Speech Situation by Determining:*

   a. When will the speech be given?
   b. Where will it be given?
   c. Who will be in the audience?
   d. What will be the subject?
   e. How will the speech be given?
   f. Why is the speech necessary?

The most important question of the six is the one dealing with the "why." If you can't find a good reason for giving the speech, take steps to have it cancelled. You can't be sincere or enthusiastic about something that isn't really necessary.

The significance of the question "why" was never more effectively (or expensively) highlighted than it was by a series of full page ads in *The New York Times,* spaced about a week apart. Each full page featured a cartoon and a slogan like: "To judge an ad, look it squarely in the Why. . . . A Whys man and his merchandise are soon parted. . . . Can you succeed in advertising without really Whying? . . . It's a rare adman who'll tell you no Whys." These advertisements cost tens of thousands of dollars to stress the "why." Think of this when you estimate a speech situation and make sure you get a definite answer to "why."

2. *Select the Subject Matter:* You should know much more about your subject than you can possibly use in your speech. This means that you must be selective about what should be included and what should not.

As I write these words I am on the island of Montserrat in the Caribbean. It is 10 P.M. I am all alone. I am surrounded by file cards, newspaper clippings, pamphlets, magazine articles, and notebooks. I must cull through this research material and decide what I shall include in the chapters of this book. This process is similar to the procedure used in selecting material for a speech.

3. *Make a Speech Outline:* Arrange the selected material in a logical order. After you have done this, walk away from it. Return after a few hours and review it critically. Rearrange it as required. Leave it again. Return and write the outline according to the best arrangement of material. List the main points and the sub-points clearly. A day or two later, review the outline and rewrite as required.

4. *Rehearse:* Using the outline, rehearse the speech. Try to simulate the actual speech conditions as closely as possible. If you can get into the actual room, do so. Make sure you time yourself accurately. Try to get someone to act as an audience. If you cannot simulate the speech conditions you are going to meet, then improvise. Sir Winston Churchill used to rehearse in the bathtub. I have rehearsed speeches on the subway by holding the outline in my hand, picking up the first point, closing my eyes, going over the words without saying them aloud, opening my eyes, getting the next point and repeating the process. I have rehearsed in my automobile. I have rehearsed in my home. During the Korean War I was taking a Methods of Instruction course at Fort Eustis, Virginia. My son Malcolm was three years old. He was the only one I could rely on to serve as my audience for the short talks I had to prepare. As long as Mal looked at me, I knew that I was speaking effectively. As soon as his eyes began to stray I would turn up the enthusiasm —pound the table—and he was an attentive audience once again.

Continue to rehearse until your familiarity with the speech outline and the accuracy of your timing convinces you that you are ready. Only if your rehearsal is satisfactory can you approach the speech with true confidence.

5. *Inspect the Place of the Speech Shortly Before the Speech:* Leave nothing to chance! Make sure that everything you require is present and is in working order. Try to anticipate what may be distracting to the audience, then take steps to eliminate or prevent such distractions.

Examples of Good Preparation

Before his final television debate with President Ford in 1976, Jimmy Carter left nothing to chance with his rehearsal and final check. Six hours before the debate, he visited the actual room where it would be held. He stood where he would be standing that evening. He had four members of his staff sit in the chairs that the panelists would occupy. These substitute panelists then questioned him, and he answered just as though millions of people were watching on television. Charles Mohr of *The New York Times* said that "Mr. Carter is one of the best rehearsed politicians in memory." If a candidate for the presidency of the United States attaches that much importance to rehearsal, how can any speaker fail to include it in his preparation? The fact that Jimmy Carter became president indicates that he must have been doing a lot of things right during his campaign. One thing is sure, he prepared for his speeches and debates properly and it paid off. Emulate his efforts to insure good preparation and you will take a long step toward making more effective speeches.

How the Kennedys Prepared

Included in the mass of newspaper clippings piled around me at this moment, there are four interesting pictures of Jack, Bobby, and Ted Kennedy. From 1958 there is a picture of Senator Jack Kennedy dressed in an academic robe sitting on a stone wall making last-minute changes to a speech he gave at a Brandeis University graduation ceremony. From 1963 there is a picture of President Kennedy making last-minute changes to his speech as Henry Ford 2nd introduces him to a business group. From 1968 is a picture of Senator Bobby Kennedy making changes to his speech as Mayor Lindsay was addressing a group in New York City. From 1976 is a picture of Ted Kennedy preparing a speech on an airplane during a five-state tour in the Democratic primaries; his wife Joan sleeps at his side. These pictures reflect the importance that three dedicated politicians attached to preparation.

Three other interesting pictures show former Prime Minister Macmillan preparing a speech in a business suit with his briefcase open beside him, President Johnson delaying a news conference in order to polish up his opening remarks, and Senator James Buckley in a crowded storeroom to which he retreated to review his speech before going to the auditorium.

A Novel Use for a Rest Room

One prominent office holder with whom I had frequent contact, would always arrive at least fifteen minutes early for a speech and ask, "Where is the men's room?" There he would go over his speech outline, assured of no serious interruption. After the first encounter with this somewhat unorthodox preparation technique, we always made sure that we had a clean, well-lighted, ventilated, and un crowded men's room ready for the principal speaker.

The Technique of Pope Pius

To give you an idea of the speaking workload of some of the world's leaders, in one year Pope Pius XII delivered 108 speeches in seven different languages. I had the

opportunity to see a sample of one of his speech manu-
scripts which showed that nine out of ten lines had been
radically changed in the Pope's own handwriting!

The Technique of Billy Graham

Billy Graham conducted a crusade at Madison Square
Garden which lasted four weeks. Every night I was in
the audience studying and analyzing how Dr. Graham
held the attention of almost 20,000 people. Each night I
changed my seat selection; I moved from the main
floor to each of the balconies, to the 49th Street side, to
the 8th Avenue end, to the 50th Street side. Finally, I
found the spot I considered most valuable for my research.
High above, and a little to the rear of Dr. Graham's speaking platform, I set up my speech "laboratory." I brought
my binoculars and followed Billy's outline as he delivered
his sermons. It was an enlightening and valuable experience. Reverend Graham had a looseleaf binder in which
his sermon was contained. The outline was prepared on a
bulletin-size typewriter, double-spaced. On each page
were notations which enriched the talk. For example,
there may have been a notation in red ink made in Bom-
bay, one in pencil made in Berlin, one in blue ink made in
London. One night, Billy's mother was present and she
read a passage from the Scriptures. Billy's bible which
was resting on his lap was immediately opened, out of
his pocket came his pen, and in the margin opposite the
verse which his mother had chosen, Dr. Graham made a
notation. This was preparation! For the rest of his career,
every time Dr. Graham reads that verse to an audience,
he will give it more warmth and meaning by mentioning
that his mother chose it when she had the opportunity to

share her favorite verse with almost twenty thousand people.

Lack of Preparation Hurts the Speech

Some years ago I was doing a radio show with Ray Owen, an NBC news broadcaster. During a break, I brought up the subject of effective speaking. Ray mentioned that at one time he had come close to failing a speech course. This surprised him because he was doing a great deal of speaking on radio and he felt that he should have done well. Since he had a good background in public speaking, he assumed that the course would be a pushover. Actually, this attitude hurt him because he didn't give the course the effort that it deserved. He did not prepare properly for his classwork and his performance was not up to his usual high standard.

The Technique of Adlai Stevenson

Adlai Stevenson was a politician who took his speaking very seriously. In 1956, when his defeat seemed imminent in the presidential election, he retired to his room and spent a whole hour drafting a short statement conceding victory to his opponent. The graceful eloquence which characterized all his speeches was the result of hours of preparation. He drafted, scratched out, substituted, and switched the material in his outline until it satisfied the high standard he set for his speeches.

Every speech you will ever deliver will be a reflection of the speech you prepared. Prepare well so your audience will have something to applaud.

THE "HELP" OF IMAGINATION

Over the years, I have often been tempted to add another *must* to knowledge, sincerity, enthusiasm, and practice. Since imagination is the element that can readily transform a good speech into a *truly* great speech, it would appear to be a likely prospect for the *must* category. On close investigation, imagination failed to qualify—not because it wasn't important, but because not all people can use it equally well. Everyone can get knowledge, everyone can be sincere or enthusiastic, and everyone can practice. But not everyone can use imagination as well as others.

Almost every large company or government agency has a suggestion program. They even offer prizes. How many employees make suggestions? What percentage use their imagination? The answer to both questions is a small figure indeed. Some employees go through their entire careers to retirement and never make a single suggestion. Very often they have an imagination but they don't know how to use it because they never tried.

The Army's Attempt to Develop Imagination

Fort Belvoir, Virginia, is the home of the Army Management School. This school is designed to "unstick" the imagination of its students. Its courses are structured to afford complete and uninhibited academic freedom to the students as they search for ways to actuate their imaginations, to achieve creative thinking. Two things about this Army program are significant: first, the importance it attaches to imagination; second, the assumption that Army personnel have imaginations which can become "unstuck."

Those who wish to speak effectively should attempt to unstick their imaginations. When you are scheduled to deliver a speech, try to use the most imaginative means possible to make it effective.

Using Imagination in the Classroom

During the Korean War, I was assigned to teach the General Orders to a group of recruits. If you have ever been given a lecture on this military subject, you know it can be deadly dull. I determined that my lecture would be different; I unstuck my imagination and went to work. Little did I dream that the product of my imagination would affect my whole life!

Looking over the General Orders, I found that each one began with the preposition *to* followed by eleven different verbs. I theorized that if we could fix these eleven verbs in the minds of the men, the rest of the General Orders would flow naturally and would be easy to recall.

The list of the prepositions and verbs looked like this: to take, to walk, to report, to repeat, to quit, to receive, to talk, to give, to call, to salute, and to be. (Though I haven't had the occasion to list these words in at least fifteen years, I was able to list them without referring to a note by imagining myself back in the room in which the class was held.)

I visited that room before the class. It was an old service club with a fireplace in front and a flight of stairs leading up to a balcony. I made three signs with the words TAKE, WALK, and RECEIVE, THEN TALK. I put a sergeant behind a desk in the back of the room and another assistant in the back with the RECEIVE, THEN TALK sign.

After the class assembled, I impressed them with the importance of the General Orders; then I gave them these instructions: Each man, one at a time, while the rest of the class watched, left his seat. He went to the TAKE sign to *take* a piece of paper that told him to report to the sergeant. The WALK sign had an arrow pointing in the direction *to walk*. When he got to the sergeant, he had to say very loudly, "Private (his name) *reporting.*" The private, noticing the sergeant is asleep, then said even more loudly, "I *repeat,* Private (his name) reporting." When the sergeant still failed to respond, the student loudly proclaimed, "I *quit.*" This was the signal for the assistant to come out and give the private his discharge. The private *received* the sign, read RECEIVE, THEN TALK and started *to talk* about the fact that he was discharged. He ran over to an open window, put his head out, and saw that the building was on fire. After giving the *alarm* by yelling "Fire!" he then ran upstairs and *called* "Corporal of the Guard." As he came down the stairs, he turned toward the chimney and noticed an officer's cap on a clothes hanger: he *saluted* it. He then put his head into the dark of the chimney to remind him *to be* especially watchful at night.

A prize was given for the best performance, which added to the enthusiasm and fun. As the men became more involved, the impression of the lesson became all the deeper.

My commanding officer entered the room on a routine supervisory visit. He remained five minutes, watched, listened, then left without saying a word. As a result of the visit, he wrote a letter that became part of my permanent personal file, commending me for imaginative and superior teaching ability. He wrote that he had been in the Army over thirty years and was never able to remember his General Orders. After watching our role-playing exercise for five minutes, he was sure that he would never forget them. As the result of his letter, I received an instructional assignment and have continued teaching to this date. Every time you speak to an audience, there is the possibility that you may make an impression that will enrich your future. This possibility is worth that little extra effort and imagination.

The Technique of Bernstein

Leonard Bernstein gave a music appreciation lecture to children in Carnegie Hall that was a classic in imagination. He told the youngsters seated at ground level that they would be the brass part of the orchestra. The first balcony was the percussion section and the second balcony was the strings. He demonstrated to each group how to make a sound that resembled the instrument they represented. He then had each section practice its sound separately. He then blended the sounds into a musical pattern. In this way the youngsters had the feeling of being part of an orchestra as they learned how its music was played.

Imagination and Traffic Education

New York City's traffic safety problems were my principal concern for about a year. To make my talks live, I used a little imagination. Instead of stating flatly that one person dies every minute as a result of automobile accidents, I tore a match out of a book of matches—then without a word, lit it. While the wondering audience watched, I wet my fingers with saliva, shifted the match to the wet fingers, and let it burn to the very end. Raising my eyes from the last flicker of the match to the audience, I said slowly and dramatically, "While that match burned, someone died in an automobile accident."

During lectures on traffic safety, the statement is

often made that many people die in accidents when they travel at high speeds because their reaction time prevents them from stopping before the crash. Because the term "reaction time" is not commonly used, we always took time to explain it. In order to vividly demonstrate exactly how reaction time worked, I asked a member of the audience to assist us. Requesting him or her to hold the thumb and index fingers about an inch apart, I then took a dollar bill and let it hang from my fingers. I would then suspend this bill between the person's thumb and index fingers at about the halfway point of the bill and instruct the person to catch the bill as soon as he saw it start to drop from my fingers. (To liven up the demonstration, I sometimes informed the volunteer that he could keep the dollar bill if he caught one.) After a half-dozen of the bills slipped to the floor without being caught, the message got across. The reaction time (during which the eyes told the brain that the bill was moving and the brain told the fingers to close) was graphically emphasized. This technique of using imagination gives a talk added interest. In the future, try to unstick your imagination.

THE "HELP" OF USING FACTS, EXAMPLES, QUOTATIONS

When a dedicated baseball fan watches a game, he keeps score of all the runs, hits, and errors. When I listen to a good speaker, I also keep score. On a piece of paper, I keep a record of facts, quotations, and examples. When the speaker says something like, "Last year 908 people were killed in accidents," I put a mark under "Facts." When he quotes someone, I put a mark under "Quotations." When he says something like, "For instance, when the astronauts landed on the moon . . ." I put a mark under "Examples."

Since I started "keeping score" about twenty years ago, I have never encountered a good speech that did not have at least one mark for every two minutes of speaking. In other words, the good speaker used at least one fact, quotation, or example every two minutes. In some cases, my score card showed a mark for every minute! This happened on September 22, 1961, when Billy Graham gave a twenty-minute sermon in Philadelphia and my score card showed twenty marks.

Examples

By using examples, you make your talk live. Dean Ormond Drake, New York University, used to call these "chunks of life," and he encouraged his students to use them as liberally as possible.

New York City affords great opportunity for exposure to great speakers at very little cost. During a period when I worked in Manhattan, I attended a service in a different church or synagogue almost every week. The denomination of the religion was not so important to me as were its speakers. For example, at Riverside Church one Sunday morning, I listened to Reverend McCracken. He claimed that he had gotten the idea for his sermon a year before. In ten minutes, he used six examples—all gathered during his year of compiling material. The sermon was excellent.

A Quotation

Since we are dealing with quotations, please permit me to share with you one of my favorites.

If we work upon marble, it will perish
If we work upon brass, time will efface it.

If we rear temples, they will crumble to dust.
But if we work upon men's immortal minds,
If we imbue them with high principles,
With the just fear of God and love of their fellowman,
We engrave on those tablets something which no time
*   can efface,*
And which will brighten and brighten to all eternity.

—Daniel Webster

This is an inspiring message for all who are privileged to come before an audience and who are given the opportunity to affect the thinking of each individual who makes up that audience.

Facts

Under the heading of facts, we often use statistics. There is nothing duller than a speaker who cites number after number ad infinitum. We realize that technical speeches may include a great many numbers that cannot be dramatized. However, if possible, try to make numbers come alive. For example, instead of saying that there were 1,452,623 people injured by automobiles last year, you could say, "If they laid all the bodies of all the people injured last year in a straight line, they would reach from New York to Chicago and back again!" Try to make the audience *see* that double line of bodies.

Instead of saying that organized crime grosses a billion dollars a year in the United States, it would be much more striking to say, "If we piled thousand-dollar bills, one on top of the other, as high as the Washington Monument; then we continued the stack two hundred feet higher, we would finally reach the total gross of organized crime for one year." On this organized crime statistic, it would also be hard-hitting to say, "If someone started spending a thousand dollars a day on the day Christ was crucified, and continued spending each day until the present time, he would not have equalled the amount grossed by organized crime in only one year." This method of presenting statistics forms a picture which makes a deep impression.

A Source for Facts, Quotations, Examples

Books are written to provide ready-made facts, quotations, and examples. *The Public Speaker's Treasure Chest,* by Prochnow, contains facts, quotations, definitions, jokes, colorful phrases, similes, and witticisms. This gives credence to our claim that great speeches should not be without them.

Collect Facts, Quotations, Examples

You will enjoy using facts, quotations and examples as much as your audience will enjoy listening to them. However, before you can use these interest-generators, you must collect them. Slip the appropriate folders into your file (the file we talked about when we discussed "Knowledge"), then fill them with facts, quotations, and examples.

THE "HELP" OF A SPEECH OUTLINE

When you give a talk, you should not be tied to a manuscript which forces you to read every word. Nor should you appear without notes, thereby forcing yourself to improvise as you proceed without direction. You should use an outline and be guided by its key words.

Horace put this principle into true focus when he said,

"Think not in words, think only fact and thought, and crowding in will come the words unsought." In other words, when you do your research, you amass a great wealth of material. During your preparation, you read it, review it, select the items to be used, edit those items, then choose certain key words to represent each fact or thought. When you come to each fact or thought in your outline, it conjures up all the related knowledge. Then you simply transform the knowledge into words and speak them in a sincere and enthusiastic manner.

Recording Notes of the Speech

People use different methods of recording their notes. Some put them in a looseleaf notebook—an excellent method because it permits additions, deletions, or substitutions. This technique also protects the outline and permits a bulletin typewriter to be used to enlarge the size of the facts and thoughts therein.

Another widely used method of recording notes is the utilization of index cards (3 × 5 or 4 × 6). The principal advantage of these cards is their compact size: They can be carried in the speaker's pocket. On the platform, they can be placed on the lectern or carried in the palm of the hand. They can also be rearranged easily. The order of the cards can be altered if it is desirable, or certain cards can be removed in order to shorten the speech. I have used this method and found it to be practical, versatile and effective.

Mental Notes

Wherever possible, you should employ mental notes. For example, if I were lecturing on what an Army recruit must know, I would want to include the General Orders.

On my outline would appear, GENERAL ORDERS–SERVICE CLUB. These four words would cause me to recall the role-playing exercise described in detail when we discussed "Imagination." Automatically the mental notes of "to take, to walk, to report," and so on, would come to mind and they would permit me to speak for several minutes without referring to a written note. These mental notes relating to the eleven General Orders are tied to a soldier's trip around that service club from the "Take" sign until he put his head into the chimney.

Your mental notes could also be linked by either a *chronological* chain of events or an *association* method of some type.

Mental notes might be tied to an *acronym*. When we discussed "Preparation" we indicated that you should estimate the speech situation. We then said you should consider the when, where, who, what, how, and why. Let's assume that we want to use an acronym to remember these six words. After examining each of them, we find that five of them begin with the letter "W," so we can't make a distinctive and easily remembered acronym out of the first letters. However, when we look at the last letters, they are all different and they spell NEOTWY. If I were lecturing on preparation, one thought in my outline would read, "Estimate—NEOTWY." NEOTWY would deliver "wheN, wherE, whO, whaT, hoW and whY" to my mind, and I would speak for several minutes without written notes.

A Word of Caution

Although mental notes give you confidence and impress the audience, you should be aware that an interruption or distraction could break your train of thought and you might not be able to get back on the track again.

Therefore, when you plan to use mental notes, include their substance in your written notes so you can refer to them in an emergency.

Prompting Devices

Since the advent of television, prompting devices have become extremely sophisticated. The old "idiot cards" have been replaced by electronic masterpieces that feed the speech automatically. These devices augment or take the place of notes on the lectern, thereby freeing the speaker from the need to look down at his notes and adding to the naturalness of his delivery.

Versions of a Speech

Some perspicacious student of effective speaking observed that there may be four versions of the same speech— the speech you prepare; the speech you give; on the way home, the speech you wished you had given; and the next day, the report of your speech carried by the newspaper. If your speech outline is poor, these four versions will differ greatly. If your outline is good, the prepared version will closely resemble the versions that follow.

THE "HELP" OF A GOOD OPENING

In 1961, I was placed in charge of a safety education program to improve the street-crossing habits of millions of New York City pedestrians. When the campaign was over, a review of its results showed that the most significant achievement was the favorable reception accorded to our activities by the street-crossing public and the newspapers. The positive response of the public and the press was due to the two words, "Excuse me." Please let me explain.

Before the program began, I met with the fifty police officers, five sergeants, and one lieutenant who would be enforcing the traffic laws in the midtown area of Manhattan. Also present were two of my actors who were to play the parts in two playlets designed to show the right and the wrong way of issuing a summons. Officer Snafu approached the jaywalker by saying, "What's your hurry?" A heated argument ensued, bodily contact occurred, and an unnecessary arrest was the unfortunate consequence. After this sorry display of police/public relations, the second playlet was introduced. Officer Eveready then took the stage and approached the same jaywalking pedestrian with the words, "Excuse me." After a "Yes, officer?" from the civilian, Eveready asked for identification, advised the pedestrian of his offense, then issued the summons to a chagrined but cooperative citizen.

I advised the officers that they had a choice. They could use a negative approach and suffer the ensuing headaches, or use a positive approach and enjoy their contacts with fellow New Yorkers. I concluded by saying, "I ask only one thing. Make a good opening statement. As soon as you approach the person, say 'Excuse me.' After that you are on your own."

The campaign lasted for ten days and more than 5,000 summonses were served. The "Inquiring Photographer" in *The New York Daily News* asked six people who had just received a summons for disobeying the WALK DON'T WALK signs how they felt about the program. One said that the police should be doing something important like catching robbers. Five felt that the police were doing a good job, and each one realized that he or she deserved to receive a summons.

Every day during the campaign, I spoke with the police officers who were issuing the summonses. They were unanimous in their praise of the "Excuse me" opening. There is absolutely no question that this technique made the program successful.

The Important First Sentence

When people listen to a speech or read an article, research shows that they pay most attention to the first and last sentences. For this reason, you should exert extra effort to make your opening a good one.

No one would argue the fact that the *Reader's Digest* has enjoyed a great deal of success over a considerable period. Much of this is due to the skillful way in which each article is constructed. Next time you have a copy in your hand, leaf through it and read only the first sentence of each article. You will be impressed with the way these openings arouse interest.

Some Good Opening Statements

A minister, Dr. Arthur J. Brown, aroused interest with this opening statement: "One hundred years ago today, I faced an audience for the first time. Then, as now, I said, 'You're probably surprised to see one of my age speaking in public.' " This excellent opener was made on Dr. Brown's 106th birthday!

William Jennings Bryan ran three times for president on the Democratic ticket. On a speaking tour in the farm belt, he met his audience at a road intersection where the only object around was a manure spreader. He climbed aboard the manure spreader and began, "I have spoken in many halls, arenas and stadiums, but this is the first time I've addressed a group from a Republican platform."

When I am lecturing about the value of a good opening statement, I produce a piece of cardboard cut to the shape of a large egg with the word EGG lettered thereon. As I show it to the class I say, "At the beginning of any talk, don't lay an egg!" I then flip the cardboard so the other side faces the class with BOM lettered on it. I then say, "Instead, drop a BOM." With that, I drop the cardboard and, as it hits the ground, I fire a blank pistol concealed until this moment. This is a real interest arouser and attention getter.

You may be wondering why "bomb" was misspelled. You may also wonder whether BOM has any significance.

The acronym BOM stands for "*Background*," "*Objective*" and "*Motivation*." Whenever you open or introduce a subject, you should relate it to the listener's *Background*, to what he already knows, so that you move from the known to the unknown. After establishing a common ground you state the *Objective*, spelling out what the speech intends to accomplish. Then take steps to answer the listener's question, "*Why* should I listen?" You must convince the listener that he will profit from your message. If we can show him that he will learn how to avoid trouble, make more money, live longer, find happiness, achieve good health, or derive any other benefit, he will have the *Motivation* to listen.

In the future, dropping a BOM at the beginning of each of your speeches will pay rich dividends in greater audience attention and an increased response to any appeal you make for action.

THE "HELP" OF VISUAL AIDS

Research has established that people remember about fifteen percent of what they hear and about fifty percent of what they see. The subject of retention was exhaustively researched by Ebbinghaus who determined that there was a definite "curve of forgetting." We forget most in the first twenty-four hours, then less each day until we are left with the permanent impression.

A realization that an appeal to the eyes may triple the amount of information retained should encourage us to use visual aids wherever possible. Of course, you should appeal to both the eye and the ear in order to increase learning—in fact, the more senses you appeal to, the better. If you can affect the eyes, ears, nose, taste, and touch at the same time, you will have the highest rate of retention.

I Never Forget a Face!

How often do we hear, "I can't remember names, but I never forget a face." This statement indicates that the brain impression from the eye is deeper than the impression from the ear. The fact is that the optic nerve is many times larger than the auditory nerve—a good reason to appeal to the optic.

The Bull's-Eye of Instruction

If you *heard* that there is a "bull's-eye" of instruction; that it contains the words "must," "should," and "nice"; and that it should guide the instructor's emphasis, for how long would you remember this statement if it wasn't repeated? On the other hand, if you *saw* a diagram of a target with the bull's-eye labelled MUST, the next ring labelled SHOULD, and the next ring labelled NICE, you would instantaneously get a better perception. Then, if the speaker referred to the target and said, "Tell the student what he *must* know: Aim for that bull's-eye and hit it again and again with essential information. In addition, you should include, where appropriate, that material he *should* know. If you have sufficient time, you may decide to include some items that are *nice* to know. Above all, you should carefully weigh all your material and decide if it falls into the "must," "should," or "nice" category. After doing this we can give each item the emphasis it deserves. This combination of "tell and show" would make a deep and lasting impression.

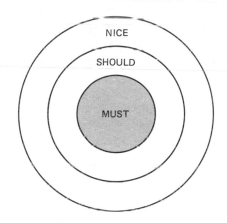

The Bull's-Eye of Instruction

You are probably familiar with that widely accepted quotation, "A picture is worth a thousand words." Shakespeare said quite the same thing in *Coriolanus* when he stated, "The eyes of the ignorant are more learned than their ears." Either quotation tells the wise lecturer to put his emphasis in visual form in order to realize the greatest response from the audience.

Appeal to as Many Senses as Possible

Our leading religions have managed to survive for century after century. Have you ever considered why attendance at a religious service is such a deeply impressive experience? Its impact is largely attributable to the fact that the service makes an appeal to every one of our senses. As soon as we enter, our eye perceives the vaulted ceiling, the stained glass windows, and the altar. Our nose identifies a smell of incense. Our ears hear a resonant organ and the spoken words from the pulpit. Our touch may be stimulated by the feel of rosary beads or a prayer shawl. Our taste buds respond to the sacramental wine. It is no accident, in an atmosphere like this, that the message preached has a marked influence on the congregation. Profit from this religious example; when you face an audience, appeal to as many senses as you can.

Feedback from an Exhibit

The use of visual aids and exhibits generates reaction from the audience, and the speaker benefits from this feedback. During a lecture on narcotics to a group of high school girls, the lecturer permitted six pills to be passed from student to student so they would become familiar with their appearance. Counting the pills to make sure all were returned, the speaker found he had seven instead of six! This feedback told him the girls were more familiar with drugs than he had assumed. than he had assumed.

Visual Aids for the "Musts"

When I lecture on effective speaking, in addition to many other visual aids, I have one sign reading KNOWLEDGE, one SINCERITY, one ENTHUSIASM, and one PRACTICE. On the back of each sign is an adhesive. Before each lecture, I ask the class to slowly shout the titles of the four *musts*. As the class announces each *must*, I put the appropriate sign on the wall in the front of the room. These cards remain on the wall throughout each lecture. Wherever possible, I refer to them. At the end of the course, by constant display and repetition, the *musts* become an ingrained part of the student's approach to effective speaking.

THE "HELP" OF MENTIONING NAMES

To the average individual, the mention of his name in a positive manner is the sweetest sound in the English language. I flew to Buffalo in January of 1969 to address a middle management class on effective speaking. Winter weather greeted our arrival with snow underfoot, six-foot icicles hanging from the terminal, and sub-zero temperatures. As I stepped from the plane, I suddenly felt warm all over. A smiling stewardess said, "Goodbye, Mr. Mc-Cullough." She had mentioned my name and I loved her for it! There were twelve persons on that American Airlines flight; while we were en route, this young stewardess memorized each person's name, then made twelve friends for her company as we said goodbye.

Make Sure You Get the Name Right

Though you should mention names wherever appropriate in your speeches, make certain you pronounce the names correctly. If you are charged with the responsibility of introducing someone, print that person's name in large letters so you won't make an embarrassing mistake. When Robert Briscoe, Lord Mayor of Dublin, visited New York City, a testimonial dinner was held in his honor and a city dignitary introduced the honored guest. After many flattering remarks, he slowly and dramatically announced, "Ladies and gentlemen . . . The Lord Mayor of Dublin . . . Robert *Wagner.*" This city official had introduced New York's Mayor Wagner so many times, that his mind automatically delivered the familiar (but in this case, incorrect) name.

It's Natural to Care About Your Image

To prove that you, like everyone else, are concerned about your name and your appearance, please ponder these questions. When the new telephone book comes to your home, do you open it and look to see that *your* name, address, and phone number are represented correctly? When you look at a group picture in which you are included, do you look to see what kind of picture *you* took before you concentrate on anyone else? The answer to both these questions is usually, "Yes." If you are satisfied with your phone listing or the picture you took, then as far as you are concerned, the whole telephone book and the whole group picture are well done because your image in each is favorably reflected.

Mentioning Names Brings a Bonus

It is amazing what happens when you use the names of people in your audience in a complimentary fashion. The individual mentioned love you for it, and the whole audience likes you if the individual is one of their group. Through the years, I have mentioned countless names in this way.

Almost without exception, these individuals make their way to the lectern after my speech, stretch out their hands, and say something like, "Great lecture." (It was "great" largely because I included their names.)

One caution: Do not identify individuals by name and give them credit for something unless you are absolutely sure that you have all the names of all the individuals who had anything to do with the project. It is better not to mention any names than it is to inadvertently overlook a name or two and thereby arouse resentment.

Learn to Remember Names

Before you can record names in your notes for use during a talk, you must remember them. You will recall names better if you make use of three words beginning with the letters "I.R.A." These letters stand for, IMPRESSION, REPETITION, and ASSOCIATION. When you hear a name in the *impression* stage, you should be sure that you can pronounce it and spell it correctly. If you have any doubts, ask the person for assistance. Everyone is pleased to know that you display an interest in his or her name. After you have the name correctly identified, *repeat* it. In your conversations with the person, preface your remarks with repetitions of his or her name. Finally, use a little imagination, and make an *association*.

In 1964, a police officer named Fontaine befriended me in Petersburg, Virginia. I didn't have a pencil handy and I didn't want to forget his name, so I made an association. I pictured a *fountain* in the middle of Petersburg. At the top of the column of water was Officer *Fontaine* in full police uniform. This picture took only a few minutes to conjure up, but I will never forget that name for as long as I live.

Remembering Names Brings a Bonus

Remembering names can have a beneficial effect on your career. Caesar, during the Gallic Wars, knew the names of a phenomenal number of his soldiers. This made him popular and contributed to his success. James Farley who had a long and distinguished political career was known for his remarkable ability to recall names. His obituary in *The New York Times* said in part, "Mr. Farley possessed a truly compendious memory for faces and names, a total recall that visibly impressed the man who was remembered." This thoughtful practice made countless friends for Jim Farley.

THE "HELP" OF SIMPLICITY AND CLARITY

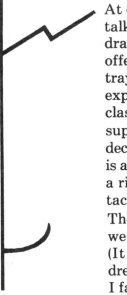

At one point during my effective speaking talks I place on the blackboard the line drawing at left. I ask the students to offer their ideas as to what the lines portray. After receiving all sorts of weird explanations. I facetiously advise the class that I was surprised that no one supplied the correct answer. "To me," I declared, "it is perfectly obvious that this is a very clear depiction of a soldier carrying a rifle on his shoulder with a bayonet attached, who is accompanied by his dog. They are just going through a door so all we can see is the bayonet and the tail." (It was "perfectly obvious" to me who drew the picture, but I confused the class. I failed to get my message across.)

Semantics

"She's fast!" Those two words to a sailor mean that a boat is tied securely. To someone at the race track, it means a horse that has a chance to win. To a dry goods salesman it means the color won't run. To others it may describe a certain type of woman.

These illustrations accent the effects of *semantics*, the science of words. They show that individuals react differently after receiving the same stimulus. Semantics is of inestimable importance to management and supervision. Unless the meanings of communications are crystal clear, there will be serious misunderstanding and confusion, not to mention a waste of time, money, and manpower. Semantics is considered so important that college courses are conducted on this single subject. When speaking, you should be conscious of the dangers of misinterpretation. You should take precautions to insure understanding by your listeners.

A good technique for improving understanding is to use short sentences. Some speakers become involved with long, run-on sentences and confuse their listeners. One of the most effective talks I ever heard consisted of six extremely short sentences. A call was received from the National Maritime Union saying that a bomb was reported to be in the building. The police responded and requested Joseph Curran, President of the NMU, to clear the building. He refused. The police official in charge went to Curran's office and made this effective talk: "Before you called the police, you were in charge. After you called us, we became responsible. We have asked you to clear the building. You refused. Now we order you. Clear the building."

A classic example of simplicity and clarity in a speech is the *Gettysburg Address*. Lincoln's choice of words leaves no doubt as to his meaning, proving that the use of long words is not necessary to be impressive. Keep it simple, clear, and concise and you will increase your effectiveness.

THE "HELP" OF REFERRING TO THE LOCALE OF THE SPEECH

"Be it ever so humble, there's no place like home." It's a fact that the average person regards with some warmth the place where he lives or works. Because of this, you should try to say something pleasant about the locale of the speech. You will add appeal to your remarks if you inject a friendly comment about the room, building, town, state, or wherever your speech is delivered.

For example, when I lecture in a certain science laboratory at St. Lawrence University I say, "When he was a student here, Kirk Douglas attended classes in this room. This means that one of you is sitting in the seat he occupied." The hard, wooden seats, especially those occupied by the female listeners, suddenly become a little more comfortable.

On many occasions, I have spoken in neighborhoods familiar to me. Because of this familiarity, I could often recall an actual fact and say something like, "Some years ago, a person from this neighborhood did something which should make all of you feel proud." After breaking the ice this way, I would go on to supply the details of the commendable "something."

In Plattsburgh, New York, I used this introduction. "Back in 1939, I came to Plattsburgh as a young infantryman preparing for World War II. Today, thirty one years later, I return to talk about another war, the war against crime."

If You Can't Say Anything Good...

Lastly, if you refer to the locale in which you are speaking, don't use a disparaging remark. Residents or businessmen may resent it, and you lose the good will of the audience. The rule to apply is, "If you can't say anything good about the locale, don't say anything."

THE "HELP" OF KNOWING YOUR AUDIENCE

There are some *general* assumptions that apply to *all* audiences. There are some *specific* facts that apply only to a *certain* audience. You should always become familiar with the background of your listeners in order to personalize your speech.

The first thing you must recognize is the combined ability of every audience: the greater its size, the greater its potential. You should respect this power. If you present your speech properly, this power can be added to the effectiveness of your talk. If you act improperly or discourteously, this power may hurt your speech.

Facing a Tough Audience

As a young lieutenant, I was directed to teach effective speaking to several hundred high-ranking officers. Each seminar was to be of three hours' duration, it would occur weekly, and twenty students would attend. The entire program was to run thirty weeks. One very concerned lieutenant (me) wondered whether he would survive to its conclusion. There were some very tough characters in the top command who might resent being asked to prepare a talk, deliver it in front of the class, then sit through a critique by some young know-it-all lieutenant. Determined to do my best and, if worse came to worst, to at least go down speaking effectively, I began preparing for the expected ordeal.

As I contemplated various options for making the course successful, I wondered how to get to know my audience better. Suddenly, an inspiration gave me hope for survival. After investigating this inspiration, my whole attitude toward my challenging assignment had changed. Despair changed to optimism, doubt changed to confidence, and reticence about beginning was replaced by an eagerness to get started.

This is the inspiration that altered everything. Our organization published a monthly magazine, one page of which was devoted to short biographies of newly promoted top administrators. By visiting our library and going back over the old magazines, I was able to compile a brief biographical sketch of each of my high ranking students-to-be. A few days before each new group arrived, a listing of its participants was delivered to me. Comparing this list with my biographical file, I blended into my material the outstanding accomplishments of a half-dozen of the scheduled students. The results surpassed my most optimistic expectations. In addition to my knowledge, sincerity, and enthusiasm, I enriched my "practice" by giving credit to my listeners. As I mentioned each name, a sparkle came into the individual's eyes, he sat up a little straighter, and the rest of the class reflected various signs of approval. After the three-hour session, I received an unexpected bonus. As the classroom emptied, a small group of top administrators came forward to the lectern, shook my hand and said in effect, "Excellent job, lieutenant." Almost without exception, this group was made up of men whose accomplishments had been recognized by me a short time earlier. Their compliment was a way of showing their appreciation for my thoughtfulness.

Stay in Your Own Backyard

Russell H. Conwell employed a similar technique many years ago. He gave the same speech thousands of times and got paid by a different community each time. His theme was always the same—to convince the audience to "stay in your own backyard" even though "the grass looks greener on the other side of the hill." He would arrive in a town a day or two before his talk and interview several of the most respected and knowledgeable individuals in the community. When it came time to make his address, he had woven the community so skillfully into the theme of his talk, that it appeared as if the talk was written wholly for this specific occasion. The people would leave the hall a little prouder of their hometown, and Conwell would leave for his next destination to weave the same kind of magic. This distinguished lecturer's success was due to knowing his audience.

Know the Individual

Whether you are talking to a thousand persons or to one, your display of interest in the listener is equally important. Paul Kilmer is an outstanding administrator. Whenever a person visits his office for the first time, a ritual is followed upon the visitor's departure. Kilmer's secretary appears with pad and pencil, and Paul dictates a résumé of what he has learned about the person. If that person returns a few years later, Paul's secretary delivers his résumé to Mr. Kilmer. After scanning it, Paul is in a position to ask about the visitor's children, hobbies, or whatever else appears on the card. Of course the visitor is favorably impressed. When you step before an audience made up of individuals, help make a favorable impression by knowing as much as possible about the audience and its individual listeners.

THE "HELP" OF BEING OBJECTIVE

Objectivity and subjectivity are at opposite ends of the spectrum. When a speaker is subjective, he speaks in terms of his *own* interests. When he is objective, he speaks in terms of his *listener's* interests. He has empathy.

A Lesson from the Bible

While Jesus was preaching, he was a prime example of objective speaking. When he talked to fishermen he used familiar terms and said, "I will make you fishers of men." They understood this language. Then when he went into the hills and talked to farmers he referred to "seed on barren soil" or "faith as small as a mustard seed." They understood. No one could dispute the fact that this type of approach had a favorable impact on the listeners.

Think in Terms of the Customer's Needs

Modern-day management is constantly striving to persuade its employees to exercise empathy: to think in terms of the customer's needs. To understand where empathy fits into our range of emotions, it might be well to examine the pathos "family." When we evoke *sympathy* we feel *with* another person. When we show *antipathy,* we have feelings *against* something. When we demonstrate *apathy*, a feeling for or against something is *absent.* When we practice *empathy*, we put ourselves in the other fellow's shoes; we *understand* how he feels. If we consider the customer's feelings and practice empathy, our sales are going to increase.

Empathy: The "You Approach"

An effective speaker should be objective. He should practice empathy. If he doesn't think in terms of the listener's interests, he will not get optimum attention. At a General Electric course some years ago I was impressed by one feature called the "You Approach" to training. This approach listed twenty-five personal goals that motivate people to do things (money, health, praise, advancement, and the like). People are naturally selfish. If we think about their wants when we prepare a speech and we take steps to satisfy our listeners' needs, then our speaking effort has a greater probability for success.

THE "HELP" OF GETTING THE AUDIENCE TO PARTICIPATE

As stated previously, people remember fifteen percent of what they hear and fifty percent of what they see. To this we add the fact established by research that people remember about eighty percent of what they *do*. If you merely *tell* an audience something, this is not very effective. If you can *tell and show*, you increase the retention. However, if you can get the audience "into the act," if you can get them *to do*, then you have achieved the ultimate in the learning process.

Learning by Doing Versus
Learning by Listening

Before I could become a colonel, I had to complete the Command and General Staff Course. I took the first half of the course by correspondence and the second half in residence at Fort Leavenworth, Kansas. A few years after, I could remember a good portion of the subjects completed by correspondence; however, there was very little recall regarding the subjects covered in the classroom. Completing a correspondence course is an active learning experience: the student *does* the work. A classroom course is passive learning: if the student merely *listens* to lectures, it is only fifteen percent effective.

Bishop John Spalding once said, "Knowledge comes of doing, never to act is never to learn." Leonard Bernstein also subscribes to this theory. Over and over again, he gets large audiences *to do* things. When he was explaining opera, he asked the audience to look at their watches and time the farewell in *La Boheme* as it was read and then as it was sung. The audience discovered that the reading took 35 seconds and the singing took 165 seconds. They participated.

In your effective speaking activity, get the audience involved. They will appreciate the participation, and your speech will be more successful.

THE "HELP" OF MNEMONIC DEVICES

A *mnemonic device* is any means employed to help a person remember something. It can be extremely helpful to the speaker who wishes to be less dependent on written notes.

Schools that feature courses on memory and concentration rely heavily on mnemonic devices. They teach their students to improve recall by memorizing an arrangement of symbols. The student ties the main points of his talk to the appropriate symbol. He can then speak without notes by running through the familiar symbols and remembering the point of his speech associated with each symbol. (If this sounds confusing, please don't be discouraged. I have put into three sentences what we worked on in a memory school for weeks. I mention it here only to inform you that such a method exists.)

On previous pages we have mentioned NEOTWY (for wheN, wherE, whO, whaT, hoW and whY), BOM (for Background, Objective and Motivation), and the "bull's-eye" of instruction. All these are mnemonic devices which could serve as a basis for a lengthy discussion without notes.

Other Examples of Mnemonic Devices

A former Trade and Commerce Minister of Canada used to wear gold cuff links with the engraving GOYBAS (Get Off Your Backside And Sell). Lecturers on administration use PODSCoRB PET (Planning, Organizing, Staffing, Directing, Coordinating, Reporting, Budgeting, Public relations, Equipment, and Training). When I lecture on problem-solving, the audience is encouraged to play it SAEF (Survey, Analyze, Effectuate a plan, Follow-up). If a supervisor doesn't satisfy the basic needs of his personnel he ROBS something from them (Recognition, Opportunity, Belonging, Security are basic human needs).

Any device you can produce to help you remember important items is worth the trouble. Let your imagination run loose. The fact is that the sillier the mnemonic device is, the easier it is to recall.

THE "HELP" OF BEING ACCURATE

Whenever you speak to an audience, be sure that your material is accurate. If you are not sure of something, don't guess. It is better to omit an item than to run the danger of being contradicted.

Don't Guess

It is sometimes difficult to resist the temptation of taking a chance on a questionable item. For example, let's assume that you are addressing an audience on the subject of traffic safety. Never before have you been so effective—you have the audience in the palm of your hand. Your knowledge of the subject is impressive, your sincerity is selling your ideas, and your enthusiasm is promoting a positive response from the listeners. As you speak, you are practicing all the *helps* to make your talk even better. A question is asked about the number of accidents during the previous year in the United States. Although you don't have the figure in your notes you remember that it was 1,408,000 and you so declare. As you do, a hand shoots up in the rear of the room and you call upon the individual who desires to speak. He rises and says, "I beg to differ with you. There were 1,840,000 accidents in the United States last year." A bit lamely you inquire, "What is the basis for your statement?" He answers, "I happen to be the head statistician for the National Safety Board—that is my basis." You say meekly, "Thank you" and the audience thinks, "The speaker was wrong! He was wrong about that item and he may have been wrong about everything else he has said in the last half hour." And so, because of one scrap of incorrect information, a great talk is severely damaged.

If You Don't Know the Answer ...

Very frequently, a question is asked for which the speaker does not have the answer. It is perfectly proper for him to state that he doesn't have the answer. In a later chapter, we will describe the different techniques for handling questions. These techniques contribute to the give and take between the speaker and the audience and add to the mutual benefits from the discussion.

If You Make a Mistake ...

If you make a mistake, and you know you made it, but the audience doesn't seem to notice it, what should you do? Go on and hope it went unnoticed, or stop the speech and go back to correct it? I suggest correcting the error is best. For example, during a speech I once said, "When we use a funny story in a talk, it should be mundane to the issue." Then I paused and I knew "mundane" didn't fit. I informed the class that "mundane" was wrong and asked them what the word should have been. Mr. De Nisco, sitting in the front row, immediately said "germane." I said, "Thank you very much." Now Mr. De Nisco felt good and my rapport with the class improved, because they recognized me as a human being who made mistakes and was big enough to admit them. Had I covered up, I might have suffered embarrassment later in the speech if someone raised the point for clarification.

When you speak, be accurate. Don't guess. If you make a mistake, admit it and correct it.

THE "HELP" OF GOOD TIMING

The peak of popularity is close to the point of saturation. For instance, if you are scheduled to give a half-hour speech and the audience knows it, timing becomes important. If the speech ends in twenty-nine minutes, you are popular. If it goes thirty-two minutes, you may have lost the audience and its good will.

Speaking Is a Privilege

To speak before an audience is a privilege and you should not abuse it. If you are given the gift of one half-hour of the lifetime of every single member in the audience, you should be grateful and show your appreciation by not going one second beyond the time limit. To do so would be to steal something precious which does not belong to you and to which you have no right.

A Sign of Good Preparation

Good timing indicates good preparation. If a person reaches his time limit without concluding his speech, this reflects poor preparation. If he had rehearsed properly, he would have tailored his talk to keep it within his allotment of time.

How Long Should a Speech Take?

If you have no time limit to restrict you, how long should your speech take? There are several light-hearted pieces of advice that respond to this question with considerable validity. The first says that the length of a talk should be like a woman's bathing suit: long enough to cover the important points but short enough to keep it interesting! Another tersely advises the speaker to, "Stand up, speak up, shut up, and sit down." Legend tells us that an Indian at a pow-wow was permitted to talk for as long as he could balance himself on one foot.

If Your Speech Has a Time Limit

If you are committed to a definite time limit, make sure you have a watch handy. Set it at twelve o'clock just before you make your opening statement. Thereafter, when you look at it you will know exactly how many minutes (and if necessary, how many hours) have passed since you started.

Whenever I come to the subject of good timing in my effective speaking lectures, I always say, "This class will be over at such-and-such hour and so-and-so minute. You have my permission to get up and leave if I talk one second beyond my time limit." No listener has ever had the chance to leave before I finished because I complete my closing statement with a little time to spare.

You'll be a more popular speaker if you don't exceed the time limit.

THE "HELP" OF APPLAUSE

Feedback from an audience is important. If questions are permitted, the speaker becomes aware of what the listeners are thinking by the content of their queries. If it is a formal speech with no questions, then the speaker must depend on other channels to assess the feelings and response of the audience.

The experienced speaker looks for many indicators, such as expressions on faces in the audience, whether the listeners are restless or quiet, whether their eyes are glued to the speaker or wandering in other directions. One of the best measures of audience reaction is applause.

Different Types of Applause

Applause is not always a sign of desirable audience reaction. Certain types of applause are less than desirable.

If applause is loud and spontaneous, that is good. It is music to the ears of a sincere and enthusiastic speaker.

If applause is of moderate volume, it is usually given as an act of politeness. The audience feels they are expected to acknowledge the efforts of the speaker and they do. This applause is not enthusiastic, it may not be sincere, and it certainly does not gladden the speaker's heart.

There are times when a speaker ends a talk and there is no applause—even from a polite audience. Applause is sometimes absent because the audience did not know the speech has ended. Of course, this is the speaker's fault and it reflects poor preparation. A speech should finish on a high note, in a manner that leaves no doubt about the fact that the closing statement has been made.

There is one kind of handclapping (not qualifying as applause) that a speaker should never cause to occur. This unpleasant sound is heard when an audience is extremely unhappy and makes its displeasure known by clapping at the wrong time. If an audience is hostile, this noisy sign of disapproval may be heard at any time. If the audience is friendly but mistreated, such handclapping might be designed to inform the speaker that he has disregarded the time limit and that the saturation point of the audience has been exceeded.

Sincerity and Enthusiasm Are Contagious!

We hope you will hear only sincere and enthusiastic applause when you speak. This will happen only if you trigger such applause by displaying sincerity and enthusiasm yourself.

THE "HELP" OF A GOOD CLOSING

While supervising the individual class presentations of sixty different instructors, I found that very few of them ever received full credit for a good closing statement. The average instructor, like a clock winding down, would say with a last whisper, "Take a ten-minute break."

Compare this sad ending of a class session with that of an effective instructor. Just before his closing statement he readies himself for his departure. Then, after a strong, well-rehearsed closing statement, he leaves the room. The class is left with the important final thought, and the class leader dismisses them for their break.

The Content of a Good Closing

A good closing should consist of a well-prepared statement that repeats the most important part of the speech. If it is appropriate, you could preface it by a summary or review of a lengthy speech. In an academic environment, it is very common to include several questions at the end of a lecture to evaluate the degree to which the lessons taught have been absorbed. In such a case, these questions would be followed by the closing statement.

A speech should not be memorized in its entirety. However, the opening and closing statements should be written out word for word and rehearsed individually until they are known well. In the introduction, the audience is getting acquainted, so you want to put your best foot forward using material with which you are completely familiar.

The closing statement should be known well and the time it requires to complete should be determined and noted. Since you must finish within a time limit, you must know when to begin your ending. Bishop Fulton J. Sheen, in his television programs, was a master of this technique. Near the end of his talk he would become more aware of the clock in the studio. At precisely the right moment, he would begin his closing statement. He would end right on schedule with the words, "God love you" and a sweeping bow.

A Quotation as a Closing

A good technique is to close a talk with an appropriate quotation. An excellent closing came at the end of a talk by a man who had devoted a great portion of his life to young delinquents with extremely bad police records. He was asked by a friend why he tried again and again, when he was disappointed so often. His answer (and closing statement) was, "Reclaim a child, and you reclaim a whole world—everyone he will ever meet, everything he will ever touch."

Rabbi Mark Tannenbaum in a radio speech was describing an act by France which brought her an immediate advantage at the expense of other nations. He closed his talk with a quote related to the expression, "laughing up their sleeves." He gave it an appropriate twist by saying that the persons responsible must be "laughing up their french cuffs."

SUMMARY

We have discussed the *helps* in relation to speech organization. After you have organized your speech, you look forward to its delivery. As the time for delivery approaches, your attitude toward the challenge becomes more evident. In the next chapter we will examine the helps to improve your attitude toward making a speech.

four
The
"Helps"
Relating to
Speech
Attitudes

If someone examined your background, he would likely find that you do certain things well and other things poorly. The chances are that you enjoy what you do well and you are not very fond of what you do poorly. Your attitude is good toward your strengths and not so good toward your weaknesses.

These observations point up the close relationship existing between attitude and performance. If you can improve your attitude toward effective speaking, better performance is likely to follow.

THE "HELP" OF BEING CONFIDENT

In 1956, Matty Imbrosciano left his home in Brooklyn to report to the New York City Police Academy. When he arrived, he was informed that because he was an expert with a pistol, he was going to be a firearms instructor. Matty agreed that he could shoot well but he was convinced that it was impossible for him to become an instructor, because he couldn't talk and lacked confidence. He said he was going back to Brooklyn. The receptionist said he couldn't leave until permission was granted. The receptionist suggested that Matty go into Captain McCullough's class for the first hour and then return to be dismissed. Officer Imbrosciano reported to the classroom.

Three days later the instructor training course ended. Matty waited in the hall until all the other students had left, then he approached me. Putting out his hand and shaking mine warmly, he said, "Thank you for changing my life. If anyone had told me three days ago that I would stand up in front of a class, and talk, and enjoy it, I would have said he was crazy." In 1968, twelve years later, I met Matty again. At one point in our conversation he said, "I have appeared on television and before all sorts of audiences. Nothing phases me. I have had groups give me a standing ovation when I finished speaking."

It may be difficult for you to imagine how a person with no confidence could change and become a very effective speaker. Yet I have witnessed this wonderful happening on many occasions.

THE BIBLE SPEAKS OF BUILDING CONFIDENCE

In the pages of the Bible, there is a record of a "student" being helped in effective speaking. According to Verse 10, Chapter 4 of the *Book of Exodus* in the Old Testament, Moses responds to the Lord when he is told that he will be a leader. Revealing a lack of confidence, Moses says, "I am not eloquent, I am slow of speech." God immediately responds with, "I will be with thy mouth and teach what thou wilt say."

Common Symptoms of a Supposed Lack of Confidence

Regarding an apparent lack of confidence on your part, you may say that you are afraid of trying, because you know you will fail. You may feel that your basic personality keeps you from being a confident speaker. You may prefer being alone rather than engaging in small talk at a cocktail party. You may consider yourself the introvert type who isn't particularly interested in becoming an extrovert. You may say that you are uncomfortable speaking with one stranger so you can't imagine how you could possibly perform well in front of a group. If this is your case, you have a great deal of company. In fact, I experience many of these common symptoms.

During my research, I have found that there are many outstanding performers who resemble you and me. Listen to this description of Sir Alec Guinness, one of the most dashing and versatile actors of our time: "He is shy and self-deprecating. He frequently covers his mouth when he laughs, can rarely look anyone in the eye, is painfully sensitive about his baldness, and talks so quietly that people who converse with him usually wind up whispering. He has a tic of shrugging that comes on whenever he is uncomfortable and he seems to be uncomfortable almost everywhere but at home and at work."

How you act in front of an audience may have little or no relationship to the way in which you act normally in your everyday activities. Hitler's landlady in Munich described him as a quiet, considerate man during the years he rented a small furnished room. He rarely talked to her and seemed to avoid conversation with others. Yet during the same period, when Hitler was in front of an audience, he was a most dynamic and effective speaker.

Richard Dilworth ran for Governor of Pennsylvania in 1962. *Time* magazine said of him: "Dilworth is basically a shy man. He feels and appears uncomfortable while partaking of that backslapping, handshaking routine. But put him behind a microphone on a formal platform and Dilworth is second to no one as a slashing speaker. Now shouting, occasionally weeping, he can carry an audience along with him on rolling waves of emotion."

An Acronym for Confidence

Please examine the word "speak." Note that it contains the first letters of *K*nowledge, *S*incerity, *E*nthusiasm and *P*ractice. If we possess these four *musts*, then *A*bility will follow and we have achieved "speak."

If you prepare properly, then approach a speaking assignment with the proper attitude you will "speak" with confidence.

THE "HELP" OF BEING YOURSELF

When we encourage students to be themselves in front of the group, they sometimes comment that this seems contradictory. One minute we tell them to be confident and enthusiastic (which is not natural for them) and the next minute we are telling them to be themselves.

Keep Your Basic Individuality

We maintain that it is not contradictory. When we talk of enthusiasm and confidence we are talking about feelings and the expression of feelings. However, when we suggest Be Yourself, we are talking about your basic personality. When your Creator made you, He threw away the mold. There is no person on the face of this earth who is exactly like you. This individuality is priceless. Keep it and cherish it, *but* take steps to improve.

When Dale Carnegie came to New York City, he had aspirations of being a star on the stage. He studied the techniques of Barrymore, Booth, and Garrick. Being of a practical mind, he reasoned that if he could take the best of each, then blend these qualities into his acting, he couldn't miss. So he adopted the speech mannerisms of one, the gestures of another, and the movements of another. When he finally auditioned, his performance was unnatural and unsuccessful. He later turned to something in which he was sincerely interested, and made his fortune teaching people to speak in public. He stopped imitating and became Dale Carnegie.

Jack Gould of *The New York Times* wrote an interesting article about the appeal of various politicians on television. He commented on the strengths and weaknesses of presidents, governors, and others. According to the people who direct television operations, the single trait of a politician's behavior that attracts television viewers the most is total naturalness.

When you speak, don't try to imitate the individual styles of successful speakers. If you act naturally you will appear more sincere. Be yourself; you will feel better and you will speak better.

THE "HELP" OF "SITUATION-SAVERS"

Many people dread speaking before an audience because they are afraid their minds may go blank for a moment and they will be unable to remember what to say. Although it is possible this might happen, no person should dread speaking for this reason. Instead, all one has to do is to accept the possibility that this might happen, then have a plan ready to handle such a situation.

Before discussing the cure, let's consider the causes. We use the plural because a countless number of things might trigger a lapse of memory: It might be a distraction that you see, hear, smell, taste, or touch; it might be strain brought on by overwork, frustration, or tragedy; it might be a physical ailment—it might be almost anything.

If a lapse of memory occurs while you are speaking, its cause is not so important as its cure—a cure to tell you what you can do to avoid immediate embarrassment and the possible destruction of the speech.

Employing the Situation-Saver

Resolve now, if you are ever at a loss for words, to employ situation-savers. These are nothing more than prepared remarks you can use in case of emergency. For example, assume you are speaking and you move away from your notes to make a point. As you approach the end of the platform, you notice a familiar face in the audience. It is the girl you almost married ten years ago! She smiles and waves to you, and your mind goes blank. You pause, look at the people in the last row and say, "If you can hear me in the rear, would you please raise your hand? Thank you very much. Now, where were we?" You return to your notes and resume speaking.

Other statements you may use to save the situation might be: "If, at any time, anyone in the audience wishes to ask a question, please raise your hand." Or, "I notice that some of you are taking notes. This is recommended for review purposes."

Another situation-saver, used by speakers whose train of thought has been disrupted, is to repeat the last part of the previous sentence until the mind clears. For example, "Vegetables are scarce and fish is expensive. Fish is expensive because it must be refrigerated. It must be refrigerated to avoid spoilage and the resultant loss of money. When money is lost, the price goes even higher." This would continue until one recovers his train of thought. The speaker who prepares properly and has his notes handy should never require this type of situation-saver. It might be required in an emergency, however, where some unexpected development prevents the use of notes.

It Can Happen to Anyone

To show that even the great suffer mental blocks, let's look at a few actual incidents. Yehudi Menuhin, the great violinist, was playing a Mozart recital in Texas. All at once he stopped, started over again and played the selection through flawlessly. After the performance a reporter asked him if he was concerned about his memory lapse. Menuhin answered that he wasn't. What concerned him more, he said, was the fact that he got stuck on the same note, in the same piece, in Boston five years earlier.

Eileen Farrell was singing an aria from *La Giaconda* when she suddenly stopped cold. A few moments later, her memory returned to normal and she finished the aria. According to Eileen, a series of frustrating incidents plus ninety-degree heat combined to set the stage for her memory lapse.

There is nothing to be alarmed about if you forget what you are supposed to say. You should accept the fact that it might happen to you. Be prepared. Then like insurance, you probably won't ever have to use your situation-saver.

THE "HELP" OF USING FOOD AND WATER PROPERLY

Every speaker has different physical needs. Some of us eat a great deal, others eat very little. Some of us drink a great deal of liquids, others drink very little. You are the best judge of what your body requires to operate at top efficiency. You are also aware of what detracts from your mental or physical performance.

Because each person is different, it is impossible to set down general rules regarding food and drink that will apply to all. However, we will discuss certain principles which should help the average person.

Common Sense and Food Habits

Do not eat a heavy meal before speaking. In your body, you have only so much blood to fill the requirements of all your bodily functions. If the demand is great in one place, there is less available for another function. If a big meal is in your stomach, the digestive process begins requiring help from the blood. This means there is less blood for the brain, your responses are slowed, you cannot perform as well, and your speaking will be hurt.

Many prominent men who are scheduled to speak at a banquet where food abounds eat lightly before they leave home. Then, instead of eating like the rest of the guests, they abstain. They use the meal time for chatting and enriching the content of their speech with facts about the organization sponsoring the affair, about the men running the organization, and about the people belonging to the organization. When such a speaker delivers his talk, he is not going to burp every few minutes. His head will be clear, and his intelligent approach to this type of speech situation produces a better performance.

Common Sense and Water

If drinking water is available, take steps to have a glassful handy. If you have it by your side you probably won't need it. But if you don't have it handy, you may run into a problem: While you are speaking, you see someone in the audience take a drink of water, and the power of suggestion makes you feel like having a drink. Then another person sips some water, and now you need a drink. Your mouth becomes dry, your powers of concentration are hurt, and you become less and less effective.

Of course, in a classroom situation where no water is available to the students, the instructor does not run into this difficulty.

The important thing about food and water is to consider it in your preparation. Make a decision how best each can serve you, then act accordingly.

THE "HELP" OF ENJOYING SPEAKING

"So this is Class 38! I have heard all about the way you behave and I am ready. Step out of line and I will see that you are suspended. . . . You! Stand up! You weren't paying attention; therefore you will be taught a lesson.

Report to the Commandant's office and wait there for me."

That is the way Lieutenant Hoover greeted our Officer Candidate School class in 1944 when we reported to him for a course in public speaking.

Lieutenant Hoover then put his head out of the door and called the student, with whom he had staged the fake banishment to the Commandant's office. Lieutenant Hoover then turned to the class and said, "Gentlemen, don't ever do a thing like that. When I ejected that student, each of you would have liked to punch me in the nose. You did not like me, therefore I had erected a barrier to communication between us by my hostile conduct."

Attitude Is Contagious

Remember that the speaker's attitude is contagious. If it is hostile the audience will be hostile. If it is friendly, the audience will be friendly. If you enjoy speaking, the audience will enjoy listening. A half a lifetime has passed since that day at OCS but I've never forgotten that valuable lesson.

A speaker's attitude is truly contagious. If he is embarrassed and uncomfortable, the audience will experience the same disagreeable emotions. If the speaker is glancing at a watch or clock wishing that the hands would move faster, the listeners will do likewise. If the speaker is disinterested or bored, his audience will feel the same. On the other hand, if the speaker enjoys speaking, his audience will enjoy listening.

Formula for Enjoyment of Speaking

You may say, "That's easier said than done. I'd like to enjoy speaking, but I can't." This is where the fourth *must* called *Practice* comes in: The more you speak, the more you learn *to make* your nervousness work for you, the more you utilize the *helps*, the more you accentuate the positive and eliminate the negative, the more you enjoy speaking.

Good preparation + good attitude + sincerity + enthusiasm = enjoyment by speaker = enjoyment by audience.

THE "HELP" OF ELIMINATING DISTRACTIONS

As a general rule, a speaker should be objective and generous. He should think in terms of the needs of his audience and he should give freely of his time in preparation. In one respect, however, a speaker should be selfish. He should insist on being the center of attraction on the platform. He should remove, or cause to be removed, anything that might distract the attention of the audience away from him or his speech.

What Can Distract

The listeners may be distracted by anything affecting any of their five senses. An offensive or an appetizing *smell* is distracting. A picture, map, or clock that can be *seen* competes with the speaker for attention. *Sounds* from outside the room, like music playing or loud talking, interfere. Dirty chairs and tables, heat or cold all affect the sense of *touch* and make the listener less likely to pay attention. These are only a few of the distractions that can arise. The speaker's responsibility is to anticipate their occurrence whenever possible and to try to eliminate them whenever they occur.

What to Do If a Distraction Occurs

If a distraction occurs, and it is of short duration, it is a good idea to stop talking and wait until the distraction disappears. This is the proper procedure because the audience will pay attention to the distraction, and what you say during its duration will be lost.

Sometimes, if it is not possible to eliminate a lengthy distraction, it may be best to eliminate the speech! For example, at a commencement exercise in Lewisohn Stadium, the skies darkened and rain began to fall lightly. As one of the speeches progressed, the rain became heavier and umbrellas appeared. Doctor Buell Gallagher, then President of the City College of New York, approached the speaker and whispered into his ear. Seconds later the speech ended.

Check for Distractions During Your Preparation

As part of your preparation, you should, before the day of your speech, visit the location where it is to be held. In addition to other things you check during this visit, look for distractions that may affect the senses of sight, hearing, smell, or touch. If you can't make the visit a day or two beforehand, arrive early on the day of your speech. Look over the arrangements quickly and make modifications where appropriate.

THE "HELP" OF USING PSYCHOLOGY

The use of psychology is somewhat like the use of imagination: Although it can improve the speech a great deal, it is not used very often by the average speaker. What do we mean by "psychology" in effective speaking? While it can take many forms, we will discuss a few.

Have Just Enough Chairs Available

If you are involved in organizing a talk, put out just enough chairs to seat the minimum number of persons expected. After these are filled, put out more as they are needed. The psychology here is aimed at both the speaker and the audience. When a speaker talks to a house that is only one-quarter full, there is a little letdown; but if every seat is taken, he feels good. Also, the closer together the audience is seated, the easier they are to control and the better their response. On the other hand, if a patron arrives after the program has started and sees half the seats empty, he may think twice about staying. However, if he sees every seat filled, he is inclined to think that the performance must be good.

How to Discourage Sleeping

A truly effective speaker is disturbed by the sight of someone in the audience who has his eyes closed and may be napping. If the speaker has responsibility for the control of an audience and he has been instructed not to condone sleeping, here is a technique I have used with great success. As soon as I see someone close his or her eyes, I ask the class to stand, stretch, and sit down. Immediately thereafter—before anyone has a chance to close his eyes—I announce, "There are many people who want to say something but they are backward about raising their hand. Maybe they don't want to be regarded as an eager beaver. Well, we're going to make it easy for you. If you want to be called upon, you don't have to raise your hand. Instead, just close your eyes. As soon as I see a pair of eyes close anywhere in the audience I'll know you want to be called upon." As I come to the end of the statement, there are a few snickers, then good-natured laughter as the audience realizes that the few sleepers will have to stay awake or be called upon.

How to Discourage Sunglasses

Occasionally you encounter some individuals who wear sunglasses; in such a case you cannot tell whether their eyes are closed or not. Here is a psychological approach for such a situation you may find helpful. For a period of five years, I put on stage productions once a week for audiences ranging from about seven hundred to two thousand. During the first performance for each new class, there were always a dozen or more pairs of sunglasses in the audience. By the second performance, the sunglasses were not to be seen.

Here's how it was done. After each playlet on the program, you would call up "volunteers" from the audience and ask them questions about the playlet just presented. These volunteers were chosen by saying, "Will the fellow in the tenth row wearing sunglasses please come to the stage?" As if by magic, more than half of the sunglasses disappeared. After the second "sunglasses volunteer" was chosen, practically all the eye shades were gone. Occasionally we found a die-hard who, even after he had been to the stage, would keep his glasses on. We would then choose our volunteer by saying, "Will the fellow to the left of the fellow with the sunglasses please come to the stage." Next, we would ask the fellow on the right to come up. About this time, the fellow in front or in back of the diehard would lean over and whisper something to him. The sunglasses would come off after the whispered advice took effect.

More Psychology

If you have a speech that is going to ask the audience to accept a controversial point of view, don't begin your speech by bluntly making such request. Instead, as Mark Antony did in his "Friends, Romans, countrymen" speech, get the audience to agree with you on several easy-to-accept viewpoints before you present them with the controversial issue. This is a good psychological approach.

When you compile a list of items that will cause the listener to be motivated (like wealth, promotion, health, happiness and the like), you are using a psychological approach. When you have a situation-saver ready in case you have a memory lapse, you are getting a psychological lift by removing a threat. If you offer a prize to the audience for any type of competition, this is a psychological technique.

How to Call for a Show of Hands

If you plan to ask an audience for a show of hands to determine how they feel about a certain question, there is a way to do it which provides a psychological advantage. If you have strong feelings concerning the question, and you would like to see it come out your way, begin by asking for a show of hands for the viewpoint opposed to yours. In other words, if you are *in support* of something, ask those in the audience who *are against* the issue to raise their hands first. People who are lukewarm about the issue will be reluctant to raise their hands. When the hands of those *in support* are asked to be raised, some lukewarm individuals will raise their hands because there is no third option to come. If it is a close vote, this psychological order of questioning may make the difference.

Use psychology. It serves to make you more interesting and more effective.

THE "HELP" OF HANDLING QUESTIONS PROPERLY

Many speakers are petrified at the prospect of being asked a question to which they do not have the answer. This is a sign of inexperience. The experienced speaker knows the value of questions, realizes that he will be asked questions for which he does not have answers, and he knows how to handle such situations when they occur.

Different Ways to Handle Questions

When a question is asked, the speaker has several options from which to choose in handling the request for information:

1. He can answer it personally if he knows the answer and does not wish to prolong the discussion.
2. He can ask the questioner what he thinks. The speaker may do this to expand the discussion even though the speaker knows the answer to the question. If the speaker does not know the answer, he gives the questioner the opportunity to supply the answer himself. Very often a question will be asked, not to find out the answer, but to afford the questioner the opportunity to display his knowledge.
3. The speaker can ask the audience what they think. Although the speaker may know the

answer, he uses this technique to expand the discussion. If the speaker does not know the answer, he is asking for the assistance of the combined intelligence and experience of the audience, which is always significant.

4. If no one, including the speaker, has the answer, the speaker should thank the questioner for bringing up the point in issue. The speaker should promise to get the answer and supply it to the questioner. The organization should also be supplied with the answer so they can relay it to the membership at their next meeting.

Don't Volunteer Personal Opinions

If possible, during your speech, try to refrain from giving your personal opinion, especially if you are the spokesman for a large corporation, governmental organization, or other sizable agency. In a give-and-take discussion with the audience, it is very easy to voice a personal opinion. Then, since you represent some agency, a listener is liable to interpret your opinion as the policy of the agency. For example, President Johnson dropped in on a luncheon his wife was having for several women to discuss the female role in the fight against crime. Unexpectedly, one of the women asked the president, "What do you think about delinquent parents who can't spend time with their children?" The president, not being briefed on the government's policy regarding this, refrained from giving his personal opinion. He answered, "I think it would be a good idea if you would ask these other ladies and then tell me what you think."

No Comment

Ordinarily, you should resolve to accept every invitation to speak. By so doing, you develop a positive attitude toward speaking that will contribute to your sincerity and enthusiasm. However, on rare occasions, it may be proper *not* to speak. Again I refer to a situation similar to the one encountered by President Johnson at the women's meeting. If, like the president, you are the spokesman for a great many people, you must be aware that anything you say may reflect on the organization you represent. If you are asked for a statement on a controversial subject, it would be appropriate to reply, "No comment." If you are pressed for a statement, it would be appropriate to say that you cannot express an opinion since you are not aware of your agency's policy on the matter.

In considering questions and discussions with the audience, the speaker who prepares properly for his speech will be well equipped. Even though the question-and-answer period is unpredictable as to subject matter, the speaker's depth of information enables him to perform creditably.

THE "HELP" OF EMBARRASSMENT

In the theatre, there is a firm belief that a poor dress rehearsal means a good performance on opening night. If, during the dress rehearsal, the curtains were closed at the wrong time, if the leading lady flubbed her lines, if a prop man put a telephone in the wrong spot, if the lighting was faulty; if any of several other mistakes were made, the experienced director or producer breathes a sigh of relief. He knows that every mistake made before opening night is not likely to be repeated during the play's first performance before an audience.

However, if the dress rehearsal goes off without a single miscue, if everyone performs flawlessly, then the director and producer worry. When the cast and stage crew make no mistakes during rehearsal, they may assume that they have everything under control and they may relax. They may not be nervous, and disaster may strike on opening night.

On the other hand, when mistakes are made during rehearsal, efforts are redoubled to prevent a recurrence on opening night. Everyone is on their toes; they are nervous and are determined to improve on the dress rehearsal.

A Wish That Certain Speeches Will Not Be Effective

At our effective speaking classes, we feature short talks by the students. Before these practice talks begin, I surprise the audience by announcing that, for each one's sake, I hope they perform poorly! I explain that these talks are like a dress rehearsal. Each student is among friends, and each wants to help the other. This is the time and place where mistakes should be made because beneficial effects are realized from each error. The person who makes the speaking blunder will not forget it. He or she will take steps to see that it doesn't recur in the future. The whole class will have had a vicarious experience with the speaker and will have profited from his "fortunate" error. Even the instructor gains added insight from each speaking mistake. To put the class at ease, we advise them that whatever embarrassment occurs in the room will remain in the room; it will not be discussed outside. Invariably, students react favorably to this approach, and a "mutual aid" attitude develops.

By encouraging the student to regard mistakes and embarrassment during a rehearsal as a valuable part of the preparation process, we hope to plant a healthy and permanent attitude toward this phase of effective speaking. In the future, when you are rehearsing for a speech and a mistake causes you to be embarrassed, we trust you will react positively. You should breathe a sigh of relief and rest assured that the actual speech will be better because of the blunders during rehearsal.

five
The
"Helps"
Relating to
Speech
Techniques

In Chapter Three we discussed the *helps* to use in *organizing* your talk. In Chapter Four, we highlighted the *helps* to improve your *attitude* toward your speech. In this chapter we examine the *techniques* to improve your speaking ability.

THE "HELP" OF GOOD APPEARANCE

In 42 B.C., Syrus the philosopher said, "A fair exterior is a silent recommendation." This is as true today as it was two thousand years ago. As I indicated on a previous page, I use a sign at the start of my classes that reads, "The audience has formed an opinion . . . and not a word has been spoken." After displaying the sign, I enumerate several things which could cause an audience to form such opinion. Appearance is one of the most important contributing factors. As soon as the speaker steps before the audience he is on display. If he presents a good appearance and his listeners like what they see, he has made a good start. If the audience is not pleased, the speaker has placed an obstacle in his path.

The Effect of Appearance

When we use the term "appearance," we mean the total visual impression given by the speaker. His physical makeup, the way he is dressed, the way he is groomed, the way he stands, the way he moves; "appearance" is everything the audience sees.

The speaker should constantly strive to improve everything visible to the audience. Although his physical build cannot be changed to any significant degree, the proper kind of attire helps. A clothes counselor at one of the better stores can make valuable suggestions with reference to the choice of clothing for a certain individual's height, weight, complexion, and other physical features. For those who are very short, it might be wise to consider the acquisition of shoes that add height. With each color, pattern, and fabric of a suit there is a best choice of shirt, tie, and handkerchief. If you are clothes conscious and you can match clothing correctly, this problem is solved. If you need assistance, get it. Don't make the mistake of getting up in front of an audience with a shocking combination which acts as a glaring distraction throughout your talk.

Uniform or Civilian Clothes?
Which Is Best?

Obviously care must be exercised in the choice of clothing. This is one reason why men who can deliver speeches in uniform have a big advantage. If the uniform fits properly, if it is clean and well-pressed, the military man, police officer, fireman, or any other man in uniform makes a good appearance. If you represent an organization, and you have the choice of giving a speech in uniform or civilian clothes, I recommend the uniform. Many corporations and companies have recognized the advantage of a standard-type dress for their employees and have adopted well-cut jackets and dresses to be worn on duty. Airline personnel are the outstanding example of the smartness of this attire and the favorable impression it makes.

De Gaulle's Technique

In 1959, when a rebellion occurred in Algeria, the head of the French government addressed his nation concerning this crisis. How did the French leader dress for this speech? De Gaulle appeared on television clad in his brigadier general's uniform decorated with the insignia he wore as a military man. This rebellion required a military as well as a political solution. De Gaulle, the astute politician, knew there was much to be gained by tailoring his appeal to the military. The impact of this television speech had deep emotional meaning for listeners who wore French uniforms because they identified with their World War II leader as he asked for their support.

"Clothes Make the Man"

In an off-Broadway theatre I saw the play *Between Two Thieves*. I was impressed with the stately appearance of Pontius Pilate. During the intermission I went out on the street to a confectionary shop. As I entered, I saw "Pilate" taking his intermission also. He was dressed in an undershirt and blue jeans. In a few minutes, his appearance had changed completely. Never before was I so impressed with the maxim that, "Clothes make the man."

Adapt Appearance to the Speech Situation

Grooming is important in certain speech situations. If a speaker is lecturing on transcendental meditation, it would be appropriate, if not desirable, for him to appear with long hair, beard, and a sari for an outer garment. The same appearance would be a drawback with another audience or another subject. Just as we adjust our vocabulary to a speech situation, so must we adapt our grooming and appearance.

Poise

Another important factor in appearance is poise. One speaker may come onstage with an armful of literature and begin to arrange it while his listeners wait. He fidgets around, puts his notes on the lectern, takes off his glasses and cleans them, puts them on, takes a sip of water, adjusts the microphone, and so on. He does not exhibit poise. Conversely, another speaker comes onstage, walks to the lectern, looks at the audience, pauses, and begins to speak. He exhibits poise. He impresses the audience favorably and he gives himself more confidence.

The Audience Likes to See the Speaker

To emphasize the importance of appearance, just imagine a speaker standing in the rear of the room, talking to the backs of the listeners' heads while they face the front. Much would be lost when the visual effect is eliminated. This is why the average person watches and listens to an important speech on television rather than on radio. Since appearance is so important, give it the attention it deserves when you give a speech. Not only will your audience appreciate it, but you will be more confident knowing that you present a good appearance.

THE "HELP" OF PROPER VOLUME

If people can't hear what the speaker is saying, they become inattentive. Such individuals then daydream, or close the eyes and relax, or busy themselves with some reading or writing, or engage in conversation with their neighbors. This last reaction is the most harmful because it is contagious. As soon as one couple starts to chat, it begins a chain reaction and pretty soon there are several whispered talks in progress.

Make Sure Everyone Can Hear

Barring hearing problems, if everyone in the audience can't hear, it is the speaker's fault. At the rehearsal, if the speech is being delivered in a big hall, the speaker should position an assistant in the farthest corners of the hall for a test. When testing, it should be realized that sound travels farther in an empty room. Therefore, if the audibility is not excellent, arrangements should be made for an amplifier.

After the actual speech begins, if there is any doubt about volume, don't hesitate to put a question to the audience. On this point, don't ask, "Can you hear me in the back?"—because if they can't, they won't be able to answer! It's better to say at the same level of volume you have been using, "If you can hear me in the last row, will you please raise your hand?"

Levels of Volume

The speaker should not constantly speak in a very loud voice in order to be sure that everyone hears. This is difficult to listen to and detracts from the speaker's effectiveness. Just as music swells and softens in order to add to its beauty, so a speech should vary in volume. The voice should be lowered to a whisper for effect, then raised above normal for emphasis. The normal volume should be just loud enough for people in the last row to hear comfortably.

If the same volume is maintained throughout, it sounds monotonous and it may put your audience to sleep. When a hypnotist is putting a subject under hypnosis, his volume is kept at the same level as he encourages sleep. Avoid sounding like a hypnotist when you are making a speech.

One thing is sure, if you remember always to be enthusiastic, your volume will change automatically and add color to your talk.

THE "HELP" OF VARYING YOUR RATE

The variance in rate that should be used normally in a speech can well be compared to driving an automobile.

Driving and Speaking Compared

When you start an automobile you go slowly to overcome inertia, then you accelerate gradually until you reach your cruising speed. When you begin a speech, you should also start slowly. In most cases, this is the first time the audience has heard you. They are becoming acquainted with your voice. A slow rate permits them to understand you right from the start and this ensures that your good introduction won't go to waste. After the first few minutes, you should employ your normal rate of speech.

After an automobile reaches its cruising speed, it doesn't maintain exactly the same speed under all driving conditions. When an open stretch of highway comes, the rate increases. On a road filled with curves, the rate drops. At a red light, the automobile stops. Similarly, after a speaker reaches his normal rate of speech, he does not maintain the same speed constantly. When he comes to relatively less important material he may speed up. When he comes to very important items, he slows down. When he really wants to impress the audience, he stops and pauses.

A speaker, by varying his rate effectively, can use this technique to let his audience know what is important and unimportant. A rate that is effectively varied provides another advantage: It sounds more interesting than a constant speed. We mentioned that the hypnotist uses a constant volume to put a subject under hypnosis. He also employs a constant rate to produce sleep. Please don't emulate the hypnotist.

Set Your Normal Rate for the Average Listener

The speaker should be aware that every audience is made up of people with different intellects. Some are highly endowed, most are average, and some are below average. If the speaker talks too slowly, the highly intelligent listeners are liable to become bored. If he talks too rapidly, the below-average listener may not be able to keep up, may become discouraged and lose interest. If the speaker uses an average rate in order to satisfy the majority of his audience, slowing down and speeding up occasionally, he has the best chance of holding everyone's attention.

THE "HELP" OF GOOD INFLECTION AND TONE

Inflection and tone give the voice personality. They provide a medium for imparting meaning, shading meaning, and sometimes changing the meaning of words. For example, if we say, "Tom is always anxious to make a speech" with normal tone and inflection, we accept it as a true statement. Now let's adopt a sarcastic tone and put a rising inflection on "always"; now the statement conveys the meaning that Tom is *not* always anxious. Now let's adopt a questioning tone and put a rising inflection on "anxious"; now the statement conveys the meaning that it is *hard to believe* that Tom is "anxious."

Anyone who listens carefully to Bishop Sheen or Billy Graham is bound to be impressed with their use of inflection and tone. Both move skillfully from a pleading tone, to a warning, to love, to questioning, to anger, to contempt, to excitement, to soothing, and so on. Each one of these feelings is reflected in the voices of these two outstanding speakers. This quality of effective speaking is largely responsible for Bishop Sheen's or Dr. Graham's ability to arouse the emotions of their listeners.

Natural Talk Reflects Inflection and Tone

For the past ten years, I have spent two or three months a year on the island of Montserrat in the Caribbean, where the people speak English. When they talk slowly to tourists, they can be understood. On the other hand, when they speak to each other, their dialect sounds like a foreign language. However, even though I can't understand a word, I have no difficulty deriving some meaning from their inflection and tone. As in America, the island's children are completely uninhibited. I sometimes park my car by the schoolyard and listen to their animated conversations. If public speakers in general had half the inflection and tone of any group of young children, there would be a marked improvement in the field of effective speaking.

Be a Little "Hammy"

The word "ham" denotes an individual who yearns to be an actor and who will perform at the slightest provocation. The average speaker would be more effective if he let himself go and became a little hammy. Instead of following a set pattern in speaking, dare to be different. Let your volume go from a whisper to a shout, let your rate go from a snail's pace to a torrent of words, and let your inflection and tone provide as much color and emotion as your speech can support.

THE "HELP" OF BEING CONVERSATIONAL

It's a funny thing: if you ask a group of students to make a two-minute talk in front of an audience, about half of them will feel as though they had been asked to face a firing squad. Yet those same individuals will go out into the hall during the break and make the greatest two-minute talk in conversation with fellow students. The key word in the last sentence is "conversation."

When people engage in a conversation they are relaxed and natural. This is how you should feel when you are speaking to an audience. If there was some means by which we could substitute an individual's conversational style for the way he addresses an audience, an increase in effectiveness would take place in his delivery. Since this proposed change is so important, we should ask the question, "Is there a way to make this substitution?"

Yes, there is a way. Next time you occupy a speaker's platform, realize that the audience is made up of individuals just like yourself. Instead of talking to or at one big audience, talk with individuals. Give each listener a piece of your conversation. Make a game of it. Try to converse with as many individual listeners as possible before your speech ends.

To Promote a Conversational Style

A good technique for promoting a conversational style is to break down the formality found in the average group of adults. Issue name cards so the group gets acquainted on a first-name basis. Remove empty chairs so the group will be seated close together. Make sure you smile whenever possible to create and maintain warmth. While you're smiling, look at individuals. Try to keep your vocal and emotional contacts on an individual basis with the listeners in the audience. Concentrate on the one-to-one type of communication between the speaker and the listener, and your conversational style will improve.

THE "HELP" OF GESTURES

In 1958, the New York City Center was in financial difficulties. The staging of *King Lear* exceeded the budget set aside for its production. Then two nights before the show opened, Orson Welles broke his leg and had to play Lear in a wheel chair. The show lost a lot of money.

There was only one chance to recoup some of the loss. Marcel Marceau, the French mime, was scheduled to appear for two weeks. He did—and played to a capacity house every night. His engagement was extended. Marcel Marceau did something phenomenal. All by himself, he transformed City Center's season from a failure into a success . . . and he did it without uttering a single word from the stage!

It was a tremendous theatrical experience to enter a theatre, remain there for three hours, then leave without hearing the slightest sound from Marceau. He didn't have to use his mouth to establish meaning. His hands, his face, his whole body evoked the impressions he intended to convey. During an interview at his hotel one day, he was asked why his gestures had such meaning and he answered, "Do not the most moving moments of our lives leave us without words?"

The Use of Gestures Is Reflected in the Voice

Every effective speaker uses gestures. This "body language" tends to make the words it accompanies more animated. To prove that gestures cause a change in the voice, we asked several students to individually read a selection twice, once with their hands in their pockets and once with gestures. We had three judges seated at the rear of the room with their backs to the speakers. After listening to each reader give his two readings, the judges voted. In every case they distinguished correctly between the readings with gestures and without gestures.

Gestures at the Start of a Speech

At the start of a speech, the speaker and the audience are getting acquainted. The rate is slower than usual, the volume is fairly stable and the gestures are subdued. In fact, it is not a cardinal sin to keep a hand in a pocket at the start (especially if this casualness will produce a conversational tone). But after the introductory remarks, the hands should be available for gestures and they should start contributing to the speech.

Although the hands and arms produce the majority of gestures, the entire body is involved in supplementing the spoken word as a means of communication. In fact, a science called "kinesics" was developed by Dr. Ray Birdwhistell in the early 1950s. In addition, books have been written about gestures. See, for example, *How to Read a Person Like a Book* by Nierenberg and Calero.[1]

The Army has a host of gestures it calls "hand signals" which have assorted meanings. They are resorted to when silence is required, when the noise of battle would prevent hearing normal orders, or when great distances permit only visual communication.

Types of Gestures

People gesture with their eyes, eyebrows, mouth, tongue, facial expression, arms, hands, feet, legs, tilting the chin, different types of smiles; in fact, research discovered more than one hundred distinct gestures of the face, hand, and body. In spite of this tremendous variety of available gestures, some speakers stand before an audience and use only their vocal chords.

At my side, as this is written, are pictures of world leaders making speeches. These were taken from newspapers and magazines over the past several years. They

---

[1]Gerard I. Nierenberg and Henry H. Calero, *How to Read a Person Like a Book* (New York: Hawthorn Books, Inc., 1971).

all have certain things in common. In every one the facial expression is animated; you can sense the sincerity and enthusiasm that the speaker feels and displays. In every one the world leader is gesturing with arm upraised, pointing to the side, pounding a shoe, clenching hands, fully extending both arms, joining hands in a praying position, jutting several fingers upwards, or pointing an index finger at the audience.

Gestures That Are Remembered

Probably the most talked about gesture in recent history was performed by Premier Khruschev of the Soviet Union. When he was addressing the United Nations, he became so enthusiastic that he took off his shoe and pounded the rostrum. On a previous page, we recommended that you ham it up on occasion. We don't recommend that you take your shoe off, but try to use some device people will remember and talk about after your speech ends.

Another gesture Khruschev used a short while before the shoe incident will live in my memory forever. Premier Khruschev attended a reception and left early. His limousine was called and Khruschev waited on the sidewalk. A boy at a window across the street switched on his record player and the *Star Spangled Banner* fell on the ears of the captive audience in the person of the Russian Premier. What did Khruschev do? He glanced at the window and saw the small boy, he stepped over to the curb, and, as though he was conducting a symphony orchestra, he gestured with both arms until the last note died. The few of us who witnessed this good-natured performance by one of the most powerful men on earth could not refrain from giving him a round of applause.

Gestures Should Be Natural

In *Hamlet*, Shakespeare refers to gestures, when he says, "Do not saw the air" and "Fit the action to the word and the word to the action." Shakespeare is advocating naturalness and this is good advice. On occasion, some speaker attempts to use "canned" gestures to be performed at the appropriate place in the speech. This is not recommended . It is reported that Woodrow Wilson, when he attended Princeton, had a chart on the door of his room with drawings of gestures. Using a device like this tends to make the speech mechanical and damages the natural, conversational effect we try to achieve.

When President Franklin D. Roosevelt spoke from a standing position, he supported his body with his arms. Since his hands and arms were not available, Roosevelt developed an effective technique of gesturing by moving his head for emphasis.

Popular Gestures

If you look back through history, you will find a gesture used at the time of Christ that has endured up to the present day. When the "thumbs down" gesture was given in the Colosseum in Rome, it meant the end of someone's life. When we make that gesture today, it signifies that we disapprove of something.

There are other popular gestures. A shrug of the shoulders with palms up means "what could I do?" Holding the nose indicates "something smells." Pointing the index finger at the temple and rotating it in a small circle means "He's crazy." Beware of popular gestures that may connote a vulgar meaning. During the 1976 presidential campaign, Vice-President Rockefeller was embarrassed when an obscene gesture that he used toward hecklers was widely publicized.

When you speak before an audience, don't depend solely on your voice. You have a remarkable body, capable of all sorts of remarkable actions. Let your body improve your speech by gesturing; it's a wonderful outlet for nervousness and you may find that you enjoy it.

THE "HELP" OF PAUSES

An interesting coincidence just occurred which I would like to share with you. Before writing about pauses I decided to take a break and walk out to the end of my porch to look out at the Caribbean. There is a hibiscus bush at the end of the porch and a humming-bird was flitting around its branches.

It darted at unbelievable speeds from flower to flower. After reaching each target, it would *pause* in midair before it put its slender beak into a blossom. The humming-bird *paused* in order to be more effective.

Substitute for "Er's" and "Ah's"

Pauses can help speakers to become more effective. An instant improvement can occur by substituting a pause for a bad habit. Back in the "Don't Worry" chapter, we talked about "er's" and "ah's." If you are afflicted with these useless speech appendages, start using pauses in their place.

A Pause Can Affect Meaning

In order to demonstrate how a pause, or the absence of a pause, can change the meaning of a statement, I would appreciate it if you would read aloud the three identically worded quotations that follow. Please pause for two seconds wherever you see three dots (. . .). Here is the first reading:

"Pardon impossible to be sent to Siberia." (If that sounded confusing to you it was, because there was no pause.) Now to the second reading.

"Pardon impossible . . . to be sent to Siberia." (What a pity, that sounds like a death sentence.) Now to the last reading.

"Pardon . . . impossible to be sent to Siberia." (Thank goodness, it sounds as if a life is saved.)

Three statements . . . same words . . . different meanings . . . all because of pauses.

Masters of the Pause

When Edward R. Murrow died, his obituary included the words, "His pauses were more eloquent than his words." During World War II, millions of Americans listened to his newscast which always began with the words, "This . . . is London." After the war his opening became "This . . . is the news." Throughout his television career, his smooth, casual style was enriched by attention-getting pauses.

When Jack Benny died, his obituary included the words, "The pauses were always more eloquent than the gags." Benny was a master of comic timing. Bob Hope also utilizes the pause in a masterful manner. Both Benny and Hope could tell a joke and not get much of a laugh. Then instead of talking they would use a pause coupled with a wondering look. The longer they paused, the louder the laughter became.

Pause Before and After Important Points

The pause is most effective when it is used before or after important points. For example, if someone asked me to sum up in one sentence the most important message in this book I would say, "Above all else . . . remember the *musts* . . . then you will have gained a great deal from this book." Note that we paused before and after the words "remember the *musts;*" this is the important thought and we wanted to give it greater emphasis.

Gary Cooper won an Academy Award for his role in *High Noon*. Few moviegoers realized why the gunfight, the climax of the picture, was a bit different from any other filmed gun duel. Throughout the entire picture, from the start until the moment when the hero and the villain faced each other on a dusty, deserted street, the theme music of the movie could be heard. Sometimes the melody swelled, sometimes it receded, but it was always there. Finally, Gary Cooper stepped out into the street with hand ready to draw. He started to walk slowly toward the showdown . . . and then the music stopped! There was a silent pause in the soundtrack for the first time in the picture and the effect was sensational. It was the pause before something important. It made the climax great.

Pause in the Proper Places

One caution concerning pauses: Don't use them after a statement that might be misinterpreted. An embarrassing example of this occurred when a woman was introducing a guest speaker. At one point she said, "I know him to be extremely capable because I worked under him for many years." She then paused. While she was pausing, someone in the audience giggled. Then it spread, and then laughter and whispering was heard throughout the audience. This was unfortunate for the woman; it was also unfortunate for the speaker.

In my thirty-six years of experience with effective speaking, the previous paragraph records the only time when a pause hurt the speech. After that unfortunate introduction, since I was in charge of the program, I asked the woman why she had paused so long. She explained that she hadn't followed her notes properly and had lost her train of thought. Better preparation and rehearsal would have avoided this mishap.

Your Pauses Will Become Effective
Only If You Use Them

Your introduction to the pause is like taking the proper golf grip for the first time: You don't feel right using it. However, just as you soon become comfortable with the proper grip on the club, so you quickly feel at ease using pauses. In your notes, mark the places at which you want to use a lengthy pause. At first you will have to insert pauses consciously. After a while you will do it naturally. When you begin to savor the complete silence of the audience during one of your pauses, and you sense the anticipation awaiting your next word, then you have taken a giant step toward effective speaking.

THE "HELP" OF GOOD POSTURE

Have you ever seen a speaker leaning on a lectern throughout his speech? If you answered in the affirmative, that means you took notice of such poor posture. My guess is that it made an unfavorable impression on you. Some listeners take offense if the speaker slouches too much because it seems disrespectful. They feel he should appear interested in his audience if not in his subject.

Over-Relaxed Posture Invites Inattention

There is a worse result connected with poor posture than a negative audience opinion. When a speaker has an over-relaxed body, it results in an over-relaxed mind which results in an over-relaxed audience which results in inattention. We must admit that a relatively fine line exists between the relaxed audience (which is desirable) and the over-relaxed audience (which is undesirable). It is a challenge to the effective speaker to identify this line of demarcation, then keep the relaxed audience on the attentive side of the line.

The Proper Posture

The proper posture for speaking is simplicity itself. You should stand comfortably erect with your weight evenly distributed on both feet. This position is the least tiring and is the most conducive to good concentration.

You should not stand in one spot for a long time unless it is absolutely essential that you do so. Such necessity would arise if you were on camera during a film or television; in such a case, being rooted in one position is understandable.

Whenever possible you should move around on the platform. When you move to the end of a stage, the listeners follow you with their eyes, and sometimes they shift in their seats. This change of position for them is relaxing. The change in perspective as a result of seeing you in a new position makes listening more interesting. Such movement benefits you because it offsets the fatiguing effect of standing in one place. More important, moving is likely to generate enthusiasm as well as some meaningful gestures.

THE "HELP" OF MANY "WE'S," LESS "YOU'S," FEW "I'S"

Throughout this book you have probably noticed how often I have used the pronoun "we." Perhaps you have wondered who else is collaborating on the book. The answer is that no other author is involved. I have used the pronoun "we" out of force of habit. Throughout my teaching career, we have avoided the first person singular "I" in favor of the first person plural "we" for the reasons set forth in the following paragraphs.

Use Many "We's"

When a speaker uses the pronoun "we" instead of "I," the audience is apt to give more weight to the statement. The consensus of a group or the policy of an organization is usually more readily accepted than the opinion of an individual. Also, if the speaker uses "we" he will not have to defend controversial statements as often. It is difficult for an audience to mount an assault on a "we" who isn't present as compared to an "I" who stands before them. You should therefore use many "we's" in your talks.

Use Less "You's"

People don't like being talked *to or at* as much as they like being talked *with*. This is why we try to achieve a conversational tone in our speeches. If a speaker uses the pronoun "you" continuously, he seems to be talking *to or at* the audience. If he uses "we" frequently, he seems to be talking *with* his listeners.

Use Few "I's"

If the speaker continually uses the pronoun "I," the audience may get the impression that he considers himself the "whole show." If the speaker uses "I" occasionally this is perfectly proper, especially if he is recounting a personal experience.

Using the word "I" almost got me into serious difficulty during the course I described back in Chapter Three when we discussed the "Help of Knowing Your Audience." Each of the high-ranking officers in that course had to give a three-minute talk during the afternoon session. To permit preparation of the talk during the lunch hour, I appeared in the classroom at 11:45 AM to brief the students. After describing what was required, I asked the students to check me with their watches while I gave a three-minute talk. After my short speech, which highlighted a personal experience, I asked if there were any questions. Without raising his hand, a deputy inspector said, "That was a rotten example; you used too many I's." This abrupt remark would have been in bad taste if only the students and the instructor were present. However, over at the side of the room observing the activity was the Commanding Officer of the Police Academy, the secretary of the Police Department, the Police Commissioner, and reporters from *The New York Times* and *The Daily News*. I was in a tight spot.

I looked at the class and smiled. I said, "Gentlemen, this is marvelous. This response represents the kind of give-and-take discussion that we hoped to achieve by the end of the week. This comment represents constructive criticism and there is no greater advocate of this than our Police Commissioner. Only last week he came into our motion picture studio to do an introduction to a training film we were making. He didn't wait for criticism, he asked for it!" I paused, and as I did a hand was raised at the side of the room. I said, "Yes, Commissioner?" The Commissioner looked at the inspector and said, "Apparently, you don't understand the purpose of the lieutenant's talk." The Commissioner then proceeded to restate the highlights of my talk. The salient points of his explanation were contained in articles carried by newspapers next morning.

This narrow escape from a speaking disaster taught me a valuable lesson. Because the incident was caused by the word "I," we always caution our students to use many "we's," less "you's," and few "I's."

THE "HELP" OF EFFECTIVE EYE CONTACT WITH EACH LISTENER

After the voice, the eyes are the most valuable tool possessed by the effective speaker. When you have a conversation with someone or when you are listening to a speech, on what do you fix your eyes most of time? If you are normal, you look at the other person's face and you concentrate on the eyes. When two people have eye contact, the effect of their communication is deepened and it is made more meaningful.

Demonstrating the Degree of Eye Contact

To emphasize to our students the importance of eye-contact, at this point in our course we conduct a demonstration. The instructor produces a pair of dark sunglasses and puts them on. Although he could still see his audience, his listeners could not see his eyes. Eye contact had been cut fifty percent and speaking effectiveness was hurt significantly. After a few minutes, the sunglasses were removed and replaced by a blindfold. Now neither the instructor nor the audience could see each other. Eye contact had been cut one hundred percent and speaking effectiveness hurt drastically.

An effective speaker draws strength from his audience. When he is performing well, he knows it because his audience tells him so. As his eyes contact listener after listener, he notes the expressions on their faces. If they reflect the message, "I can understand you perfectly, you are doing a great job, you have me sold," then the speaker knows he is getting across. However, if he is not contacting many pairs of eyes as he moves from face to face, something is amiss. It may be that the average listener has his eyes closed, is daydreaming, is looking out the window at something more interesting, or is too embarrassed to look at the speaker. Something is wrong and the speaker must apply corrective measures. In a situation like this, a remedial measure is to double your enthusiasm. When you come alive, your audience will look at you and eye contact will be reestablished.

Eye Contact and Truth Go Hand-In-Hand

The eyes are the mirror of the soul. When two persons are looking into each other's eyes, it's difficult to keep from telling the truth. During the Korean War our family lived in the village of Lee Hall, Virginia. One day my neighbor came over and told me that the valve on his oil tank had been opened and the oil had run all over his back yard. He thought my son might have done it. I located my three-year-old and said, "Malcolm, look at me."

Malcolm's blue eyes looked out from beneath a shock of red hair and met mine. I said, "Did you open Mr. Reed's oil tank?" Malcolm's eyes dropped and he began to speak. I interrupted him and said, "Mal, look at me." He did, and while our eyes held each other's, he said, "Yes I did." I don't believe Malcolm has ever told me a lie in all his twenty-seven years. It is possible that this is due to our eye contact whenever a sensitive question was discussed. When you talk to an audience, look them in the eye if you want to be believed.

An Eye Contact Exercise

When I come before a group of people for the first time, I engage in a little "eye-contact, getting acquainted" exercise. After placing my notes on the lectern I look at the audience in silence; then, with the trace of a smile on my face, I try to meet the eyes of every person in the room. If the audience is large, I do the same exercise except that I concentrate on one face in each section of the auditorium. It is not an easy matter to do this well, but the warmth it gives to my opening statement makes it worthwhile. During a talk, I will return often to a good listener; one who always seems attentive and approving. From a person like this, I draw strength. There are some persons to whom I do not return often—the few persons who fail to respond warmly in spite of the speaker's best effort.

Eye Contact Adds to the Enjoyment of Speaking

It is amazing how misconceptions concerning the use of the eyes are common among educated men and women. This was the case with a talented executive who was in one of our courses. A few months after the course ended, I was making a dedicatory address in the Washington Heights section of Manhattan and he approached me. He put out his hand and said: "I want to thank you. All my adult life I have been embarrassed every time I had to make a speech because I didn't know what to do with my eyes. Someone mistakenly advised me to fix my gaze about twelve inches above the back row and hold it there. Since I attended your class and learned to look into the eyes of the listener, I'm a changed man. Now I actually enjoy making a speech."

Eye Contact Permits Individual Conversations

We have said many times that you should try to make your speech seem like a conversation with individual listeners. Your eyes can do more to help you in accomplishing this goal than any other part of your body. You can appreciate that it would be impractical for you to leave the platform to talk to each individual listener. However, your eyes can make each and every listener feel that you are conversing with him or her personally. As your eyes travel from a listener in the left rear, to one in the middle, to one in the right front, you give a complete thought to each one. Each listener feels as though he has been conversed with personally. If the audience is large, the speaker should look at one specific face in the auditorium (it is amazing how others in the area feel that the speaker is looking at and talking to them also). I had this experience when I moved all over Madison Square Garden and I listened to Billy Graham, night after night. Wherever I sat, at some time during the sermon, I thought Billy was looking at, and talking to me. I remembered this experience about a year later when I had an occasion to speak in that same Madison Square Garden. I made sure that I gave the same eye contact to a listener in the distant second balcony as I gave to someone in the front row.

Eye Contact as a Control Device

Your eyes represent an outstanding means for controlling the audience. We have described on an earlier page the control method featuring the statement, "If you want to be called on, just close your eyes." To apply this control device, we must depend on eye contact. We also mentioned how to get rid of sunglasses in a large audience; again the eyes play a major role. Whether I'm controlling the response of only my son Malcolm or of thousands of listeners, the eyes provide the key to success.

Eye Contact Can Help You
Get a Following

Although a speaker's words have an important effect upon an audience, his eyes sometimes have a more profound effect on an individual listener. When Adolf Hitler spoke to vast audiences, there have been several listeners who have testified to the fact that Hitler's eyes met theirs at some point in his talk. They declared that in the few fleeting seconds that Hitler looked into their eyes, their life was changed. When Senator La Follette was building his political following in Wisconsin, he searched the eyes of his audience each time he made a speech in a new community. After visiting with each individual through eye contact, he would concentrate on that person who seemed most responsive. As soon as the speech ended, he would make his way to the side of the individual whom he had selected. He would then ask the person to join his team and represent him in that area.

Listen with Your Eyes

Art Linkletter made a fortune interviewing people. When asked what his secret was, he answered, "Listen hard." In other words, Linkletter's outstanding performance was due largely to the help he received from the person he was interviewing. A speaker can't listen with his ears as Linkletter did, because his audience is usually not making a sound. But the speaker can listen with his eyes. He can note the responses of the audience and be guided accordingly. If a quizzical expression appears, that is a signal for the speaker to explain the point in issue more fully. If the group looks a bit restless, it's time to speed up the rate a bit. If they start looking at their watches, it's time to take a break. If each and every eye is glued to the speaker's, that is the cue to keep up the good work.

When a movie star or a television personality wants to travel incognito, what is the simplest way to accomplish this? They usually put on a big pair of sunglasses and their appearance is changed. When pictures are taken of drug addicts to show the horror of infected limbs, the individual's eyes are blacked out in the photo and his identity is lost. More than any other part of the body, eyes reflect the key to your personality and appearance.

At our instructor training courses, after lecturing to a new group for an hour, I could almost predict which individuals would develop quickly into effective speakers and which individuals would not make rapid progress. During this first hour, I would search the faces of the eight or ten instructors-to-be. A few looked back at me with a rapt expression; their eyes were alert and they held my gaze until I moved to the next face. One or two wavered when I contacted their eyes and then they dropped their eyes because they were unable to return my look. With hardly an exception, the students who returned my eye contact warmly performed admirably in contacting the eyes of their audience when they lectured. With hardly an exception, those students who failed to permit me to look into their eyes had difficulty in learning to make effective eye contact with their audiences.

Convince Them with Your Eyes

Effective eye contact reflects sincerity. If you want listeners to accept your message, convince them with your eyes as well as your words.

THE "HELP" OF FEEDBACK

When you approach any task, there is a right way and a wrong way to go about doing it. You can approach it haphazardly with no system, make mistakes, waste time, and get few positive results; this is the wrong way. On the other hand, you can survey the situation, analyze the findings, select the best course of action, put the plan into effect, and then *follow up* to obtain information on how the task was accomplished.

This approach is similar to the preparation for a speech advocated in Chapter Three. We made an estimate, then we gathered material, then we selected the best material, then we rehearsed and made a final check of the room, and then made the speech. Note that we did not include the "follow-up" emphasized in the previous paragraph. This follow-up, as applied to speechmaking, would mean getting a feedback from the audience on how the speech was delivered and how it was received.

Encourage Feedback

A large percentage of schools and specialized courses use formal questionnaires for gathering information on how the instruction is delivered and how it is received. This data is used for evaluating the present system and for planning any required changes.

All speakers who are serious about their speech-making should have some method for getting feedback. Whether it is from a friend in the audience, from a checklist, from conversations with listeners, from a suggestion box, from your spouse, or from any other source, feedback has value and it should be encouraged.

In the educational system, various means are employed to supervise instruction and to let the teacher know how he is doing. In the Armed Forces, an efficiency report is rendered on every commissioned officer by his supervisor at regular intervals. The objective is twofold: First, if an officer knows he is being rated, he performs better; second, when he is rated, weaknesses are discussed and plans for improvement are developed.

If a speaker knows he is going to get feedback, he will very likely put forth extra effort to make the feedback favorable. After he gets the feedback, he is more likely to find out about his faults and he can take steps to correct them.

THE "HELP" OF EMPHASIS

Unless you indicate to the audience what is the important part of your speech, they won't know. Unless you take steps to make them remember the important points, they won't remember. There are many ways to accomplish emphasis; we will discuss a few of them.

Repetition

One of the finest speeches Martin Luther King ever delivered was the one which highlighted the theme, "I Have a Dream." Although its prose was impressive, the most memorable characteristic of that speech was the stirring repetition of "I Have a Dream." Repetition is one of the best means of emphasis. Throughout this book we have repeated "knowledge, sincerity, enthusiasm, and practice" over and over. This was intentional; we want you to remember the *musts* and repetition will help, whether it is written or spoken.

In 1941, I gave a first aid course to a class of air raid wardens. Throughout the course, whenever we tied a bandage I would make sure the ends of a square knot were tied correctly by repeating, "left over right; right over left." In 1959, I had occasion to return to the building where the course was held. One of the participants of the course was there and he recognized me. He didn't remember my name but he called out, "Left over right; right over left." Repetition had made an impression that lasted eighteen years.

Volume

Another excellent method of emphasizing an important point is by the use of volume. The idea is to utilize either extreme in the level of volume. Either raise your volume far above normal, or lower your volume to the point where the people in back can just about hear. At either extreme your words will be emphasized.

Pause

As we mentioned earlier, emphasis is also obtained through the use of the pause. The best method is to pause before and after an important thought.

Rate

When we discussed rate, we indicated that emphasis is obtained by slowing down your normal rate of speaking. If you have heard one of Winston Churchill's famous speeches delivered during the assault on England, you have heard a master use the slow, deliberate, measured rate for achieving emphasis.

Inflection and Tone

By using various inflections and tones, a speaker can provide color and emphasis. When he exhibits anger, pleading, warning, or some other emotion, the listener is more likely to be impressed.

Gestures

Gestures are an ideal device for emphasis. Raising the arms, pointing with the fingers, pounding the lectern with the hand, and similar motions, have the effect of action supplementing the sound of the voice.

Visual Aids

Visual aids appeal to the eye. The brain remembers about half of what is seen; therefore to show as well as to tell is a great way to emphasize.

Demonstrations

If you were to explain how to tie a shoelace in words, you would probably confuse the listener and he would remember very little. However, if you put your foot on a chair and actually tied and untied a shoelace, he would get the idea. Demonstrations are excellent for stressing the correct way of performing a physical act.

Practical Exercises

You remember about fifteen percent of what you hear, fifty percent of what you see, and more than eighty percent of what you do. Obviously the practical exercise in which the audience participates is the best way to emphasize. This is why short talks in a speech course are so important. This is why you should rehearse and speak as often as possible.

Role-Playing

The technique of role-playing is an outstanding way to impress people. Individuals from the audience are put into simulated real-life situations. They are asked to play the roles of the principals in such situations (principals can be parent/child, customer/employee, taxpayer/civil servant, and so on). By playing the role and reacting to the other person, the benefit from "doing" is achieved by the players. The audience watching the role-playing exercise gets a vicarious benefit.

An Accumulation of Emphasis

Before leaving the subject of emphasis, it may be well to demonstrate how a single piece of information in a speech can be increasingly emphasized by using various devices.

On an earlier page, we mentioned that a good beginning for a speech should contain "background, objective, and motivation." We will use this item for our emphasis demonstration:

1. *Words:* We can simply say, "A good opening for a speech should have background, objective, and motivation."
2. *Printed Matter:* If literature was distributed for the speech, we could call the attention of the audience to the place where the item is mentioned.
3. *Acronym:* We could announce that the first three letters of Background, Objective, and Motivation spell BOM.
4. *Blackboard:* We could place on the blackboard: "BOM = Background, Objective and Motivation."
5. *Sign:* We could show an EGG sign.
6. *Slogan:* "When you open a speech, don't lay an egg; instead, [turn the sign to BOM] drop a BOM."
7. *Action:* Drop sign at end of slogan.
8. *Sound:* Fire blank pistol as BOM sign hits the ground.

This emphasis demonstration is one of the high points of our effective speaking course. The student remembers this long after other things are forgotten. Twelve years after Dennis Carey had seen this demonstration, I met him at a party at 2 AM and he said, "Hey Bill, I use your BOM in every speech I make." In spite of the late hour and the liquid refreshments, Dennis remembered.

Decide What and How You Will Emphasize

Before you give a speech, decide on its most important

points. Then use a little imagination. Select one or more methods for emphasizing the important points and make a notation concerning such methods in your speech outline. Years from now, someone who heard you speak will tell you how they never forgot something you said. They will, if your emphasis makes them remember.

THE "HELP" OF HUMOR

Some people can tell a joke well; such persons should use appropriate humor often. Other individuals cannot tell a joke well; they should use appropriate humor rarely.

When we discussed "Be accurate" we mentioned that any story that is used in a speech should be germane to the issue. In other words, don't tell jokes for the sake of making people laugh. Tell jokes and stories because they relate to the subject and help you to get your message across. For example, we may be discussing the fact that you may meet an unsympathetic audience when you speak. To illustrate what we mean by an unsympathetic audience, we could use this story:

A young girl decided she wanted to become a nun. She entered a convent where she could say only two words every half-year. At the end of six months, she reported to the Mother Superior, who asked, "Yes, my child?" The young novitiate chose her two words with great care and said, "Food bad." Six months later she reported to the Mother Superior who asked, "Yes, my child?" The young novitiate said, "Bed hard." Six months later the Mother Superior asked, "Yes, my child?" The young novitiate said, "I quit." To this the Mother Superior replied, "It's just as well, you've been complaining ever since you got here." This Mother Superior was an unsympathetic audience!

THE "HELP" OF CHARISMA

"Some men are born great, some acquire greatness, and some have greatness thrust upon them." This well-known quotation could be paraphrased to accommodate the word "charisma": "Some men are born with charisma, some acquire charisma, and some have charisma thrust upon them."

Charisma is that quality which identifies a person as being something special. It cannot be defined as a set combination of certain physical, mental, and moral characteristics. It is indefinable, yet it is there. When a charismatic person walks into a room, it seems that his presence is felt by all who observe him.

Jimmy Carter's Charisma

There is no question about the fact that a high office a person occupies lends charisma to his personality. The head of a government, by virtue of his office, is accorded deference and respect not ordinarily bestowed on the average person. However, it must not be overlooked that an elected head of government came to that office largely because he had charisma. The first time I ever saw Jimmy Carter was during an hour-long interview with Bill Moyers on television. I watched intently for sixty minutes, then turned to my wife and said, "I think he'll be our next president." What Jimmy Carter said that night did not meet with my complete approval, but the *way* he said it earned my overwhelming approbation. It was because of charisma. Even on television it was in evidence and it exerted a profound influence.

161

Charisma of Other World Leaders

During my career I have seen many world leaders in person. There is no doubt about the fact that they exuded charisma. I was standing a few feet away from Fidel Castro and Nikita Khruschev when they hugged each other in front of the Russian Consulate in New York. I helped lift President Roosevelt from his car when he returned to Hyde Park in the summer of 1941. I conversed with Eleanor Roosevelt. In an official capacity, I was in company with De Gaulle, Tito, Nasser, and Presidents Truman, Eisenhower, and Kennedy. In 1944 I spent several hours with Jimmy Cagney on the *Ile de France* before he sailed on that troopship to entertain our servicemen overseas. All these personalities had charisma. All derived benefit from its presence. One of these benefits was the fact that they were more effective speakers because of charisma.

Charisma Can Be Developed

While some of these great personalities were born with charisma or had it thrust upon them, the overwhelming majority acquired charisma. During World War II, the major objective of the four-month Officer Candidate School was the development of leadership, a term practically synonymous with charisma. I can assure you that the Second Lieutenant McCullough who graduated from OCS was different from the Sergeant McCullough who entered. The symbolic difference was the fact that the sergeant saluted officers whereas the lieutenant returned salutes. Inwardly, the personality of a leader had been developed, a new attitude toward responsibility was evident, and my overall performance was improved.

Charisma and You

You *can* acquire leadership and the charisma that accompanies it. This statement is not intended to imply that you will become a leader on the national scene. It does mean that you can develop self-assurance to the point where it will be recognized by those around you.

We have placed the subject of charisma at the end of our discussion on *helps* for a reason. If you are normal, you want to impress people favorably. You will make a better impression if you are confident and self-assured. Start today on an organized self-development program. From this day forward, whenever you rehearse a speech or give a speech, please be certain that you do two things. First, constantly check to see that the *musts* are always present. Second, select one of the *helps* and make sure you apply the technique several times during the speech. By mastering a little at a time, you will build up your ability and confidence. Then will come a day when you will have added all of the *helps* to your delivery. At that time you will be an effective speaker and you will know it. You will then have acquired a measure of charisma.

six

The "Avoids" of Effective Speaking

Certain things hurt speeches and should be avoided. These things reflect unfavorably on the speaker or on the organization of which he is a part. Some of these trouble-makers can be corrected with little difficulty; the speaker is aware of their presence and takes remedial action. However, some of these troublemakers are difficult to prevent because the speaker is unaware that he is causing them to occur. Such a situation calls for a little detective work. The speaker can ask a colleague to sit in the audience and listen to his speech in order to discover anything that should be avoided in the future.

AVOID MISPRONUNCIATIONS OR
GLARING ERRORS IN GRAMMAR

The average speaker is not aware that he is mispronouncing words or that he is committing glaring errors in grammar. Only if he is told about it can he correct it.

It made me wince to hear the president of the United States mispronounce an important word over and over again. President Eisenhower pronounced "nuclear" as "nucular." It was amazing that it was never corrected. After his death, a newspaper article mentioned it, so I wasn't the only one in America who winced.

Whenever the subject of correcting one's English is brought up, we should remember the magnificent job done on Eliza Doolittle by Henry Higgins in *My Fair Lady*. We can improve greatly if we try. If you have a good education but you have adopted careless speaking habits, it's just a matter of putting your grammatical house in order. However, if the fault lies with your lack of education, I would suggest strongly that you go back to school and take a course or two in English. (I started taking courses after work in 1937. With the exception of the time spent in World War II, the Korean War, and the Vietnam War, I took courses every year until 1967. It was time-consuming, but the benefit far outweighed the sacrifice.)

AVOID PROFANE OR VULGAR EXPRESSIONS

In 1952 an instructor at Fort Eustis, Virginia, greeted his class with the words, "Good morning from Fort Uteris, Vagina." In less than an hour he had been transported to the station hospital and was awaiting an examination by the psychiatrist. A sensitive major who was in the audience was offended by the remark—she left her seat and called the Commandant's office.

The Laugh It Gets Isn't Worth the Harm
It Does

Do not use profane or vulgar expressions when you are speaking to an audience. A speaker has no right to take advantage of his position. A great many popularity-seekers indulge in this practice because they always get a warm response from the audience. There is no question that a good percentage of the average audience laughs heartily at a vulgar joke. But even if ninety-nine percent laugh and only one percent is offended, it is not worth it. The ninety-nine who laughed soon forget the joke along with the person who told it. But the one percent don't forget. In all probability, that remark of the instructor at Fort Eustis was greeted with a lot of laughter, but one person didn't laugh. As a result, the speaker was removed from the platform and his entire career was adversely affected.

Shakespeare Supports This View

Shakespeare put this caution about offending the audience beautifully when his Hamlet gave his famous "advice to the players." He said in part, "Tho it make the unskillful laugh, it cannot but make the judicious grieve, the censure of which one must in your allowance o'erweigh a whole theatre of others."

AVOID HOLDING THE LECTERN OR
DESK FOR LONG PERIODS OF TIME

When a small child is frightened, he will sometimes run behind his mother's skirt for protection. The child does this naturally; it wants to get something between him and the thing that threatens him. This fact is a psychological explanation of why some speakers do not come out from behind the lectern, rostrum, or desk. They regard the audience as a threat and they want to keep something between them and the thing that threatens them.

The Average Listener Wants the Speaker to Succeed

Being afraid is as ridiculous as it is harmful. The listeners who make up the average audience want the speaker to succeed; they are on his side; they provide support. If, instead of talking to an audience of forty persons, a frightened speaker scheduled individual interviews with each of those forty persons, his fear would probably dissolve as he chatted comfortably with each one. You will agree that there is no sound basis for being afraid of something made up of friendly parts. Throughout this book we have encouraged the speaker to regard his speech as an expanded conversation. When you are on the platform, don't make a speech to one big audience; instead, talk with each of the individuals in the group with the aid of eye contact.

Regard Individual Listeners as Friends

If you regard the audience as a threat, you cannot be effective. Your attitude is reflected in your voice, as well as in your actions and your whole being. But if you regard each listener as a friend, and you sincerely and enthusiastically try to reach each one with your message, you will find yourself out from behind the lectern trying to get as close as possible to your friends in the audience.

Move Out After Your Opening Remarks

During your introduction, it is perfectly proper to stand behind the lectern or desk. In your opening remarks you are becoming acquainted with each face and each individual is becoming acquainted with your voice and the BOM of your speech. However as soon as you finish your opening remarks, you should move out from behind the lectern as often as you can.

When I was a young boy, my uncle used to take me to boxing matches. One of my favorites was Kid Gavilan. If the Kid fought a ten-round fight, he would employ a different style in almost every round. One round he would be in a crouch, next he would be erect, next he would move to the left, next he would move to the right, next he would lead with his right, next with his left. He was marvelous to watch because of this variety. If he plodded out of his corner every round in the same way, he would be just another fighter and I wouldn't be telling about Kid Gavilan's artistry more than forty years after I saw him. When a speaker moves around the platform, he presents a different picture to the audience, he is more interesting to watch and listen to, and his speech is more effective.

Don't Lean on the Lectern

If someone stands behind a lectern all the time, he invariably starts to lean on it. Out in Suffolk County, New York, I placed my notes on a shaky lectern and noticed a sign, "Please don't lean on the lectern, it may collapse." Speeches throughout the country would improve if every lectern had a similar sign reading, "Please don't lean on the lectern, your *speech* may collapse!"

The speech may collapse for this reason. When the speaker leans on the lectern, his body becomes relaxed, his mind then becomes relaxed, the audience becomes over-relaxed and, finally, the audience becomes inattentive. In essence, the speech has collapsed.

Use a Microphone Which Permits You to Move

Another item which tends to make a speaker take root in one spot is a fixed microphone. Because the microphone can't move, the speaker doesn't move. If you must use a microphone, request that a lapel microphone be made available. Make sure you rehearse with the lapel mike so you become familiar with handling its extension wire. When President Johnson changed to a lapel microphone for his press conferences, the newspapers commented on how much more effective his delivery became.

AVOID PLAYING WITH THINGS

When I lecture, I wear Ben Franklin glasses. They are half the height of normal eyeglasses and they allow the wearer to look out over the top of the frame. They permit me to read my notes, then to look directly into the eyes of individuals in the audience. Before changing to this type, I tried bifocals without much success. Before that, I used ordinary glasses which were completely unsatisfactory. I would put them on, refer to my notes, take them off and speak for a few minutes than I would put them back on, refer to notes and then take them off. This was disconcerting, it tied up a good gesturing hand, and worst of all, it was difficult to avoid playing with the glasses. Speakers whirl them, fold and unfold them, insert them and extract them from their pockets, and so on. If you happen to use eyeglasses, don't distract your audience by playing with them.

The Ring Twirler

J. Wesley Lyle was scheduled to give an important speech in Delaware. He asked me to listen to his final rehearsal. During my critique I asked him if his ring was bothering him. He answered, "No, why?" He was surprised to hear that he kept twirling the ring on his left hand with his right hand throughout the entire fifteen-minute speech.

The Handkerchief Wiper

John Glendale was giving a lecture one day and I sat in to observe. John is one of the finest instructors I have ever known. You can imagine my surprise when John took out his handkerchief, wiped his mouth, and put away the handkerchief—every few minutes. This repetition continued until the conclusion of his talk. As soon as I was alone with John, I asked, "Why do you keep wiping your mouth, is it bothering you?" He asked, "What do you mean?" I told him what he had been doing. John was completely unaware of his distracting movements.

The Button Opener and Closer

Bernard Schechterman lectured to our Army unit at the University of Miami. While speaking, he opened the button of his jacket, put his hand in his trouser pocket, took out his hand, closed his jacket, dropped his hand, opened his jacket, put his hand in his trouser pocket, took out his hand, buttoned his jacket—for half an hour. Next day I met him on the campus. I complimented him on his excellent talk; then I asked him if he realized what he was doing with his jacket button. He said he didn't, so I told him. He then said, "Now I understand why that button fell on the stage during the class after yours yesterday!"

The Chalk Tosser

Some speakers use the blackboard and do not put down the chalk. They sometimes toss it into the air a few inches and catch it. They also sometimes drop the chalk and don't bother to pick it up. As they move around, the audience is watching their feet waiting for them to step on it.

The Pointer Bender

Another favorite plaything is a pointer. After the speaker has used it to point to a map, chart, or graph, he doesn't put it down. He sometimes holds it by the two ends and bends it a little; then he bends it a little more. Pretty soon the audience is waiting for the snap.

Keep Your Hands Free

When you lecture, don't let your hands hurt your speech by playing with things. Keep them free so they can gesture and make your delivery more effective.

AVOID PACING BACK AND FORTH

During the U.S. Tennis Open at Forest Hills, I was seated in the marquee at the center of the playing area. Looking out across the court, I could see most of the fifteen thousand seated spectators in the background. As the ball went back and forth across the net, I was amused to notice how its flight was followed by thousands of heads moving to the left and right in unison.

Such a side-to-side head movement by an audience watching a speaker pace back and forth on the platform is not amusing. It is tiresome and disconcerting. The speaker is experiencing a healthy nervousness but he is wasting it. Instead of using this nervousness to be enthusiastic and to gesture, he is using the harmful pacing technique as an outlet. He looks more like a caged animal in the zoo than an intelligent speaker.

Move with a Purpose

When you speak, you should move with a purpose. For example, you move from your notes to place something on the blackboard. You put down the chalk, step to one side and discuss what you placed on the blackboard. You then return to your notes for a few minutes, then leave them to perform a demonstration. You return to your notes, then move to the left end of the stage to give the audience a new perspective. And thus you vary movements in this way until the end of your talk.

We mentioned earlier that Kid Gavilan was a great fighter because of his variety of movement. You can be a better speaker if you move often—and move with a purpose.

AVOID MEMORIZING A SPEECH

To memorize a speech is to play with dynamite. If you forget one word, it will throw you off and you may not be able to continue.

In fact, you don't have to be guilty of forgetting a word; you can be completely innocent and still meet disaster. If, in the middle of a memorized speech, someone's chair collapses, or an urgent message is brought to the stage for someone in the audience, or someone raises his hand, or any interruption causes you to stop, you are in serious trouble.

When we say "avoid memorizing a speech," we mean that you should not memorize the entire speech. It is perfectly proper—in fact, it is impressive—to recite a quotation without reading it word for word. As Bishop Sheen did, knowing your closing statement close to memorization is often effective. But the bulk of your speech should be extemporaneous. From your condensed outline, you pick up a fact or thought and extemporize; you develop it naturally in a conversational tone.

Effective Speaking and Effective Listening

Just as courses are given in effective speaking, so are courses given in effective listening. The course in effective listening teaches you to hear a great deal, then to reduce this great quantity of sentences and paragraphs into a small number of key words. Actually, an effective speaking course advocates a procedure diametrically opposite. We start with a small number of key words in our speech outline, and we expand it into a great quantity of sentences and paragraphs.

Extemporize, Don't Memorize

The quotation by Horace relating to this subject is so appropriate that it bears repetition, "Seek not for words, seek only fact and thought, and crowding in will come the words unsought." In other words, use notes and extemporize—don't memorize.

AVOID READING YOUR SPEECH

Unless it is impossible to do otherwise, it is insulting to read a speech to the audience for at least two reasons:

The first reason is related to the fact that it is a great deal easier for the reader to read the speech word for word than it is to speak the speech in the proper manner. When the speech is read, the reader is saying in effect, "I didn't care enough for this audience to prepare properly. I didn't research in depth, didn't make an outline, didn't rehearse, didn't do any of these things because I didn't think this audience was worth the effort."

Second, the reader is insulting the intelligence of the audience. He is implying that the audience can't read properly therefore he will do it for them. If a person intends to read a speech, at least he should give the audience an option. He should pass out copies of his speech at the door, then, if an individual wishes, he can go home and read the speech at his leisure. If someone needs help with the reading, he can sit and listen.

A General Bores His Audience

At a graduation ceremony I attended, a brigadier general delivered the commencement address. His subject was one in which he had a lifetime of experience, his military career. I could hardly believe my eyes and ears when this general began reading his speech. He continued to read, hardly ever lifting his eyes. for almost twenty minutes. The speech was deadly dull and reflected unfavorably on the military profession.

When Reading Is Necessary

There are times when the reading of a speech is necessary. This is the case when newspapers, radio, and television are quoting what was said, word for word. In a case like this, there is no margin for error and the speech must be read in order to prevent costly misunderstandings.

President Eisenhower, during his talks on television, afforded the students of effective speaking a valuable lesson. He would read word for word for a few minutes. Then he would pause, take off his glasses, look out into the living rooms all over America and restate, in Ike's natural, conversational tone, what he had just read. The difference in effectiveness between the reading and the speaking was enormous. The reading was dull; the speaking was sincere, enthusiastic, and enjoyable.

If You Have a Choice

If you ever have a choice of reading or speaking the speech, remember your audience. You owe it to them to make the speech as interesting as possible, therefore, avoid reading the speech.

AVOID ALCOHOL

"If you drink, don't drive; if you drive, don't drink." We hear this excellent advice regularly. We could paraphrase this to read, "If you drink, don't attempt to make a speech;

if you have to make a speech, don't drink." This is also excellent advice.

Alcohol Is a Depressant

The reason why you shouldn't indulge in driving or speech-making while you have alcohol in your system is related to your reaction time. Your reflexes are slowed down and it takes longer for you to react. In an automobile, it may mean death. On a platform, it is almost certain to cause embarrassment; in an extreme case, it may mean a wrecked career.

Dry Martinis Instead of Proper Preparation

At a large trade convention, a salesman was scheduled to make an important demonstration for his company. He had never taken a course in effective speaking nor had he ever read a good book on the subject. He couldn't avoid the speech and he didn't know how to proceed. As the hour for his demonstration came closer, well-meaning friends gave all sorts of advice. One suggested a dry martini and the salesman quickly headed for the bar. One martini made him feel so relaxed that he had a second and a third. A short while later, he began his presentation. The demonstration was a complete fiasco because of his intoxicated condition and his lack of preparation. This failure was embarrassing to the salesman, to the company he represented, to the audience, and to the sponsors of the convention.

Alcohol Destroys Nervousness, and That Is Bad!

To speak most effectively, you should be stimulated and sensitized by nervousness so that your senses are sharpened and your responses quickened. Alcohol is a depressant and it has the opposite effect of nervousness.

If you drink, don't make a speech; if you make a speech, don't drink.

DEPENDENCE ON FUNNY STORIES

Please note the first word, "dependence." You should depend on knowledge of your subject, belief in it, and eagerness to tell about it. If you depend on funny stories, the objective of the speech is lost and it becomes a case of amusing the audience rather than informing them.

Don't Get a Reputation as a Comedian

If you depend on funny stories, you will get a reputation as a comedian. People who come to listen to you will expect to be entertained. You will have to live up to your reputation. If you speak to the same people frequently, you can't use the same jokes. If you can come up with new jokes regularly, you belong on television. The best solution is to use funny stories sparingly.

As we mentioned on an earlier page, your funny stories should be germane to the issue. If the story doesn't relate to the subject and doesn't help sell your ideas, it should not be used.

AVOID ANNOUNCING YOUR SUBJECT
WITH YOUR FIRST WORDS

"I am going to talk about . . . "—how often we hear speakers say these words followed by the title of their talk. When these are the first words directed to the audience, it represents a grievous error in speaking technique. Let's consider why this is so.

Before a speech begins, the majority of the audience is engaged in conversation. Some of these conversations are concluded in whispers as the speech opens. Others who were conversing are not whispering, but they are thinking about the last remark prior to the beginning of the speech. As a result, the speaker is lucky if he has half of the audience listening as he starts his speech. In view of this, if the speaker announces his subject immediately, only half the audience receive an impression from the words.

Out of the fifty percent who receive the impression, a good percentage may not care for the subject and they may be lost. The remainder, those who don't have strong feelings against the subject, may not be inclined to listen because the speaker failed to motivate them sufficiently.

Giving the Listener Time to Shift His Concentration

Announcing the subject in the very first sentence is a very common error, sometimes committed by experienced (but not very effective) speakers. When we discussed "eye contact," I mentioned that I indulged in an exercise to try to meet the eyes of every person in the audience before I speak the first word. By doing this, I establish contact with the individuals and I give them time to get their pre-speech conversations out of their systems and to shift their concentration to the speaker.

Instead of Announcing Your Subject at Once, Use "BOM"

The subject of your speech should be announced when you have optimum attention. This is why the BOM formula is so valuable. You establish common ground by discussing *Background,* then you announce the *Objective* (subject), then you *Motivate* the group to listen.

AVOID ANTAGONIZING THE AUDIENCE

Antagonism acts as a barrier to receptivity. If you ruffle the feathers of the audience, don't expect them to accept what you are trying to sell. If the audience has been offended, the speaker must make amends before good rapport is restored.

Antagonizing an Audience May Be Unintentional

Unfortunately, the speaker sometimes fails to realize that he has offended the audience. Most of the time it is unintentional. But, intentional or unintentional, the harm is done and the sensitive individuals in the audience become resentful.

In 1954, our acting group was performing a playlet to demonstrate how an officer should report sick. I asked Sergeant Patrick Murphy (later Commissioner, Police Department, City of New York) to be the desk officer. After the playlet, we entertained questions from the audience. One young man asked, "Why did the desk officer have to sound so annoyed?" Neither Pat nor I realized that he had used this tone of voice. However, one listener objected to it and it is very possible that others in the audience may also have been antagonized.

Reasons for Audience Antagonism

Since the speaker is usually unaware of offending the audience, it is a good idea to become acquainted with the kind of remarks that might turn an audience off. Here are a few: any indication that the speaker is prejudiced against any race, religion, nationality, or political belief; any profanity, vulgarity, or objectionable terms; any unwarranted sarcasm about a sensitive subject; any derogatory statements about popular persons, places, or things.

Be Tactful

Make it a rule to use tact. An excellent maxim states, "If you can't say anything good, don't say anything." For a speaker who must speak, and who should speak tactfully, this saying might be restated as, "If you can't say anything good, try to find a reasonable substitute." For example, if you want to say something nice about a woman's face that is so ugly it would stop a clock, the tactful way to get this message across would be, "Madam, when I look into your face, time stands still." Same message, different approach.

Keep the Audience on Your Side

Delivering a speech effectively is enough of a challenge without complicating matters. Keep the audience on your side; don't antagonize your listeners.

AVOID APOLOGIZING FOR SPEECH

When a speaker opens his talk with an apology, it is a form of rationalization. By apologizing, he is excusing himself for what he expects to be a poor speech. It is not surprising that the usual result is, as expected, a poor speech.

By apologizing, the speaker throws a roadblock into his own path. It is like a fish peddler yelling, "Stinking fish" as he tries to sell his wares. Who is going to buy what he is selling after he says it stinks?

Examples of Bad Openings

Here are some examples of apologetic openings (which should never be used):

"This is a dry subject but I'll make it as interesting as I can." (He fails.)

"I have only one hour to cover a whole day's work." (The audience gives up.)

"Our subject today is very difficult, but I'll try to make it as clear as I can." (He tries, but fails.)

"They didn't give me much advance notice, I haven't had much time to prepare, but here goes." (And there goes the audience . . . more "stinking fish.")

When an audience hears apologies like these, they lose interest and occupy their minds with more important or more pleasant thoughts.

Resist the Temptation: Don't Apologize!

In the future, no matter how tempted you are to apologize for your talk, don't do it! Instead, take the material you have and sell it with sincerity and an overabundance of enthusiasm. Don't be surprised if people come up when you finish and say, "Great speech!"

AVOID FALSE CONFIDENCE

Just as "pride goeth before a fall," so false confidence precedes an unsuccessful speech.

A graduate student at Queens College was scheduled

to give a talk. The assignment didn't faze her because she had successfully given a speech on the same subject only a month before. She was confident that she would repeat her success. Because she did not prepare properly, her speech was a failure.

This speaker's confidence was false confidence, characterized by an absence of nervousness. The speaker doesn't experience nervousness because no fear or anxiety is felt regarding the speech. The speaker is not concerned about the outcome because he or she never considered the possibility of failure.

Confidence Should Stem from Proper Preparation

A speaker should be confident. However, this confidence should stem from a realistic appraisal of the speech situation. He should realize that any speech can fail if it is poorly prepared and/or poorly delivered. Being aware of this fact helps provide the motivation to succeed. By applying the principles of good preparation as set forth in this text, *true* confidence is possessed by the speaker as he approaches and delivers his speech

THE POWER OF EFFECTIVE SPEAKING

If you analyze the characteristics of world leaders, of men considered great, you find that they seem to have very little in common. Some are tall, others short; some are thin, others fat; some are old, others in the prime of life; some are well educated, others have little formal training; some are benevolent, others are tyrannical. It is difficult to find any trait that a majority possess. That there could be an attribute which almost every world leader has in abundance is almost unthinkable, yet such is the case. That necessary ingredient of leadership is the power to communicate, the ability to speak effectively.

The noted author and historian, Bruce Barton, phrased it well when he said, "In my library there are over ten thousand volumes of biography. They all tell the same story. More men have achieved success by their ability to speak, than through any other skill. Effective speakers have always ruled the world. The wise thing to do is join them."

More than fifty years ago in Germany a young radical set out to dominate the politics of his country. His principal (if not his only) asset was his ability to speak effectively. He achieved his goal, then attempted to rule Europe and Africa. In Germany he was thought a saviour; throughout the rest of the world he was considered a despot.

In the next chapter we will analyze Hitler's career to learn how his speaking ability helped him to gain the power used to bring about the rise and fall of the Third Reich.

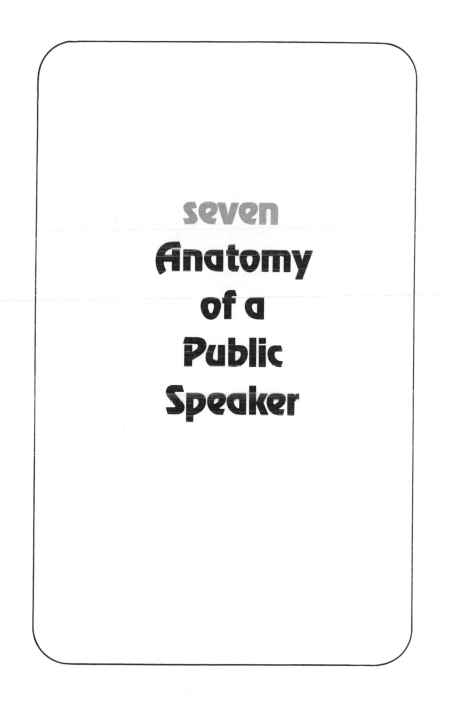

seven

Anatomy
of a
Public
Speaker

During the twentieth century, no political career was more closely tied to effective speaking than that of Adolf Hitler.

From 1945 to 1948, I served in the Office of Military Government, Wuerttemberg/Baden, West Germany. For more than three years I was exposed to the awesome consequences of Hitler's dictatorship. I was deeply involved in destroying the remaining vestiges of the Nazi organization. Two days a week I sat as a judge in court, trying cases involving Germans. Many of these cases were based on the actions of the accused in supporting the aims of Hitler. One day a week I sat on a Denazification Board which determined the disposition of properties controlled by former members of the NSDAP. I attended the Nuremberg War Crimes Trial and observed Goering, Hess, and other close associates of Hitler. In my official capacity, I reviewed hundreds of books dealing with the Hitler regime. I talked with many government officials and prominent Germans who gave me an insight to the Hitler personality.

Hitler's ability to speak persuasively was the key to his success. By virtue of his remarkable skill in impressing audiences, he was able to control the population of Germany and to aspire to world domination.

How did Hitler do this? What speech techniques did he employ in his rise from obscure politician to world leader in fifteen short years? To find the answer, let us examine Hitler's public speaking activities. We'll start by determining whether the Nazi leader possessed the *musts* of effective speaking.

KNOWLEDGE

During the year he spent in Landesberg Prison, Hitler wrote the book *Mein Kampf,* the blueprint of his beliefs and aspirations. This book reflected the knowledge Hitler was to use in his political speeches. He lived and breathed the making of a Germany in his image; when he spoke about this, he certainly had knowledge.

SINCERITY

Hitler's sincerity had a profound effect on his audiences. Early in his career, people came to heckle him but remained to listen and be swayed by Hitler's sincerity. On several occasions, people have testified that their lives were changed after seeing and hearing Hitler for the first time.

His sincerity was a prime factor in prompting people to adopt such a new way of life. His burning zeal and sincerity in preaching his Nazi gospel caused an adoring population to liken him to some kind of deity.

ENTHUSIASM

Hitler had abundant enthusiasm and he eagerly sought the opportunity to lecture on his favorite subject. When he spoke, he electrified his audiences; they became part and parcel of his animated delivery. His voice, his gestures, his expressions; everything about his forceful style heightened the impact of his words. Because of Hitler's enthusiasm, his listeners became enthusiastic. In speech after speech, his admirers shouted themselves hoarse. Their *Sieg Heil*'s were an ever-present characteristic of his aroused and responsive audiences.

PRACTICE

Hitler practiced. As a very young man, he left his work if there was an opportunity to address a group. As a budding politician in Munich he spoke in the streets, in beer halls, or in any other location where he might recruit followers for his cause. As a national figure, he frequently addressed the German population. As a world threat, he continued to make speeches. Throughout his career, he practiced effective speaking.

Undoubtedly, Hitler had knowledge, sincerity, enthusiasm, and practice. He had the *musts* which guaranteed effective speaking. Now let us look at some other aspects of his speaking techniques that added to his effectiveness.

PREPARATION

At the start of Hitler's speaking career, he doubted his ability to speak effectively. He set out to improve. Hitler attended public meetings and studied the manner in which they were conducted. He observed the techniques and measured the effectiveness of the speakers. He learned a great deal about what to do and what not to do.

Hitler prepared his speeches carefully. If the occasion had special significance, he would labor over the content of the speech. He would make an outline of his speech and use this for a guide and reference during the actual speech.

Hitler rehearsed his speeches by the hour. Words were not his only concern. He concentrated on his appearance and body movements. It is believed that he rehearsed before a mirror in order to achieve the effect he desired.

ORGANIZATION OF THE SPEECH

As a rule, Hitler began his speeches quietly. After determining the mood of the audience, he adopted the speaking style to best accomplish his speech objective. Invariably, his delivery became more rousing and more emotional as the speech progressed. It ended with a mutual display of unbounded enthusiasm by the speaker and the audience.

PSYCHOLOGY

When Hitler was speaking to small groups in Munich, he made his meetings lively. The atmosphere was sociable. There were beer and snacks and music. Then, at the most opportune moment Hitler appeared and began his appeal for support. Later on, when he travelled from place to place, he asked for information regarding the audience he was to face. Based on the makeup of the crowd, he produced from his suitcase a record with appropriate music. This record was played to provide the proper prelude to the inspired message of *"der Fuehrer."*

CLARITY

Hitler took pains to present his points clearly. He was understood by the common man in the audience. In the farthest corners of a hall he was as audible as he was to those seated in the front rows. In a speech containing several points, he paused after each one to ask if the meaning was clear.

EYE CONTACT

Hitler had clear blue eyes, and he used them well. There are many recorded accounts of the highly-charged emotion experienced by individuals when their eyes contacted those of Hitler. Many have stated that this brief visual encounter had a profound impact on their lives. Hitler's listeners saw honesty and sincerity in his eyes. Of course, this feature contributed greatly to his remarkable success as a speaker.

CONFIDENCE BEFORE AN AUDIENCE

In private conversation, Hitler did not always make a great impression. However, when he came before an audience, his power to communicate became impressive. He was a prime example of the fact that many people are much more effective before a group than they are when dealing with individuals. Before an audience, Hitler was inclined to be enthusiastic, active, and forceful; in normal conversation he was generally quiet. Hitler drew strength from the audience; the bigger and livelier it was, the better Hitler performed.

GET THE AUDIENCE TO PARTICIPATE

In the NSDAP organization, there was something for everyone. For the children there was the *Hitler Jugend*; for the teenager there was the *Arbeitsdienst*; for the men and women alike, there were dozens of societies; and even for the elderly there was a service to be rendered. As Hitler spoke to audiences, he invited them to participate. The people accepted and identified with the movement. People came to listen to Hitler as individuals; when he had finished speaking, there was a spirit of unity and comradeship.

FEEDBACK FROM AUDIENCE

Hitler observed his audience carefully when he spoke. If he paused and didn't hear a sound; if he asked a question and got an immediate response; if he searched the facial expressions of his listeners and found acceptance, he was gratified and was spurred to greater effort. This close relationship with his audience had an effect on Hitler's demeanor. In front of an audience he was more assured, more aggressive, and more emotional then he was when carrying out everyday activities.

INFLECTION AND TONE

Hitler ran the gamut of emotion in a speech. He exhibited hate, fear, anger, love, pleading, indignation, humor, or pity. When each of these was displayed, his voice and facial expression and body movement reflected such emotion. This variation of inflection and tone made Hitler's speeches more effective.

CHARISMA

Edith Herman lives in Montserrat, West Indies, where I talked with her about Hitler. She heard Hitler speak at the Tempelhof Stadium in 1934. She had no use for Hitler but she attended to hear and see the man she disliked. She was far from the speaker's platform while Hitler delivered his speech. "Yet," Mrs. Herman said, "in spite of my animosity and in spite of the distance which separated us, Hitler mesmerized me." By virtue of his consummate skill as a speaker, Hitler had developed a charisma which was greatly in evidence when he occupied the speaker's platform. This charismatic quality was heightened by the contrived use of music, flags, banners, uniforms, and lighting. For example, when Hitler spoke at Tempelhof before a hundred thousand spectators, every single person sat in darkness. The only lights were those that illuminated the lone figure of Hitler as he delivered his speech.

GESTURES

Hitler used his body to heighten the effect of his words. He appreciated the value of gestures and he worked to improve their execution. His use of body movements was almost theatrical because he planned and rehearsed certain gestures to be used to produce a certain response from the audience. When he clenched his fist, or stretched out an accusing finger, or raised his arm slowly, or pounded the lectern, there was no disputing the fact that the gesture added to his effectiveness.

REPETITION

It is a rule of propaganda that if you repeat a lie often enough, it will be accepted as true. Joseph Goebbels, Minister of Propaganda, worked closely with Hitler on his speeches, using the technique of repetition often. Hitler made repetition more dramatic by employing it rhythmically. In a society where slogans were at every hand, Hitler's use of repetition infused his audiences with catchwords and phrases to be remembered.

NOTES

Hitler used notes in outline form for his speeches. He referred to his outline, picked up the next cue word, then extemporized as he developed the thought suggested by the word or phrase. His speeches were built soundly and logically, and he delivered them in keeping with his planned outline. It is interesting to observe that Hitler used glasses when he was out of the public eye; however, a photograph never showed him with glasses nor did he wear them when he spoke in public. This means that his notes must have been in large print in order for him to see them without the aid of glasses.

SUMMARY

Hitler's speaking career could be regarded as having followed a normal pattern. He was unsure of himself at the outset but he developed into an outstanding speaker by the application of sound techniques. He fortified himself with a wealth of knowledge, he believed wholeheartedly in his subject, he was eager to tell about it, and he spoke as frequently as he could throughout his entire career.

Hitler's speaking career was also extraordinary. He was highly motivated and extremely capable. His rise to international prominence was directly related to his ability to speak effectively.

Before concluding our chapter on Hitler, we would like to make one point clear. We realize that Hitler's ideas and policies were evil and that they ultimately led to his self-destruction. Our discussion was not concerned with the tragedy which he brought upon the world. Our sole intent was to present an evaluation of Hitler's ability to speak effectively.

eight
Methods
of
Instruction

At some time in his career, almost every speaker becomes responsible for instruction. It may be in a formal school environment, or it may be an informal course given to a small group. Because it is very likely that you may be called upon to conduct lectures in a course of instruction at some time in the future, you should be acquainted with those essential elements if you are to fulfill such a requirement.

WHAT PRODUCES EFFECTIVE INSTRUCTION?

In order to understand what produces effective instruction, many factors must be considered: the student, the facilities, the theory of instruction, the techniques of the facilities, the theory of instruction, the techniques of instruction, and, most important of all, the instructor. Each of these areas will be discussed, starting with the theory of instruction. We will begin by analyzing the answer to the question, "What makes people learn?"

WHAT MAKES PEOPLE LEARN?

There are some very obvious answers to this question. With regard to the intake of liquid by a student, we all accept the fact that some liquids aid learning and some inhibit learning. For example, two ounces of coffee stimulate the average student while two ounces of whiskey seriously harm his powers of concentration. Obvious examples like this are well-known and we guide ourselves accordingly.

However, many not so well-known factors affect the way people learn. To these relatively unfamiliar elements we address ourselves. We refer to the way in which learning is affected by:

1. the background of the student,
2. the objective of the speech,
3. motivation,
4. actually doing while learning, and
5. learning under realistic conditions.

These five items are *principles of learning*; we will discuss each of them.

1. Background

Every audience you face is different. Each has a different background and it is up to you to determine its composition. After you have made such a determination, you can capitalize on this information. You can gear your teaching approach to best build upon the background of the audience.

The instructor should make use of what the listener already knows. He should move from the known to the unknown. He should relate new material to familiar material. By considering the background of the audience, he or she can draw on their experiences for illustrations and examples. The instructor should use reviews frequently to ensure understanding of past instruction before presenting new material.

2. Objective

To maximize learning, students should be told what they should expect to achieve during each specific hour of instruction. This aim, objective, or goal should be spelled out clearly. It should be related to what is expected of the student. In considering the objective, we should think of it in terms of building blocks. A course has an objective, and every hour of instruction within that course has its own individual objective. As each objective is achieved, the student experiences a sense of accomplishment.

Every hour of instruction therefore contributes to the achievement of the overall goal and builds toward the course objective.

3. Motivation

By motivation, we mean a desire on the part of the listener to try to achieve the objective. Sometimes this motivation is present before the speech begins. In most cases motivation must be developed in the listener; this is a challenge for the instructor. There are many ways in which the instructor can instill motivation. Let's look at some of these possibilities.

Personal Benefit: Most certainly, motivation is developed if we can show the listeners that they are going to derive a personal benefit if they absorb the key principles of the lesson to be taught. If the instructor can convince the listeners that they will make more money, be healthier, avoid trouble, or realize any other personal advantage, then those listeners will be motivated to pay attention.

Recognition: A listener is motivated to learn if he gets a pat on the back from the instructor. If he does something correctly and the instructor recognizes this, a positive attitude on the part of the listener results.

Instructor's Effectiveness: The instructor's effectiveness affects motivation. If he is listless and boring, the desire to learn lessens. However, if he is sincere and enthusiastic, motivation is enhanced and the desire to learn grows.

Basic Human Needs: Every human being has certain needs. He feels a need for belonging, for security, for opportunity, and for recognition. If the instructor can satisfy any of these needs, then the listener is motivated in a positive manner.

Competition: Many individuals are highly competitive. They enjoy nothing more than a contest of some sort. If the instructor can employ a teaching activity to capitalize on this desire to compete, then positive motivation results.

Negative Feelings: Just as we strive to achieve positive motivation, so we should strive to avoid feelings of the negative type. Care should be exercised to avoid any word or action that might generate adverse feelings or an emotional barrier to learning.

4. Doing

People learn best through actual experience. If they can personally perform the operation, then they remember a great proportion of what was taught. People retain about fifteen percent of what they hear, about fifty percent of what they see, and about eighty percent of what they do. Wherever possible, the instructor should devote time to practical exercises in which the student performs.

5. Realism

Teach in a realistic manner. Stay on the level of the listeners. Don't insult them by a presentation that is too elementary; similarly, don't discourage them by talking over their heads.

Teach in Terms of Ultimate Use: Teach the material as it is to be used by the listeners. If you are teaching effective speaking, relate the material to the actual performance on the speaker's platform. If you are teaching a manual skill (piano, accounting, typing, for example), get the actual tools of the trade into the classroom. If the student can play the piano or make entries in ledgers or type on a typewriter, then his training is most realistic and most profitable.

Summary

If we consider where the listener has been (background), tell him where he is going (objective), convince him that he will benefit from the instruction (motivation), permit him to participate (doing), and teach the material as it is to be used (realism)—then we have maximized the degree of learning experienced by the student.

From Theory to Practice: Now that we have considered the factors that heighten the learning process, let's turn our attention to the recommended procedures for carrying out the actual instruction.

STAGES OF INSTRUCTION

We will discuss five stages of instruction:

1. the *planning stage* in which we prepare the material to be presented,
2. the *telling and showing stage* in which we present the material,
3. the *performance stage* in which the student applies the knowledge presented,
4. the *examination stage* when a check is made on the degree of absorption of the material presented, and
5. a *review stage* which permits the participants to discuss the material presented.

1. Planning Stage of Instruction (Preparation)

In this first stage of instruction we prepare the material to be presented. We begin by making an estimate of the instructional situation. We come up with answers to questions concerning when and where the instruction will be held, who will be involved, what will be presented, how the instruction will be given, and why the instruction should be given.

Research, Speech Outline, Rehearsal, Final Check: After the estimate is satisfactorily accomplished, we research and select our subject matter. When this is complete, we use such material as a basis for the organization and formulation of our speech outline. The next step is to rehearse. Finally, shortly before the actual presentation, the last check should be made of the facilities and the equipment to be used for the presentation.

2. Presentation Stage of Instruction

The presentation stage has three parts:

    a. the *introduction,*
    b. the *explanation,* and
    c. the *summary.*

Each of these parts contributes to the objective of the presentation stage which is to tell and show.

A. Introduction Part of the Presentation

The introduction sets the stage for the entire presentation and prepares the listener for what is to come. This is where you should use the BOM: The introduction should consider the listener's background, set forth the objective of the instruction, and furnish motivation to heighten the desire of the student to learn.

Length of the Introduction: Occasionally, the question is raised as to the length of time an introduction should take. There is no hard and fast rule; however, a reasonable estimate would be about ten percent of the length of the speech. In other words, a half-hour speech should have an introduction of approximately three minutes. More important than the length, is the content of the introduction. It must get attention, arouse interest, and convince the listener that the message to be delivered has a great deal of significance for him.

B. Explanation Part of the Presentation

The explanation part of the presentation stage deals with the new material to be transmitted to the student. In this part, the instructor employs the best means possible to explain the content of the lesson. Although the lecture is the most popular method, the instructor might decide to use the conference, panel discussion, demonstration, motion picture, chart, exhibit, or any other teaching technique.

Rules for Applying Various Teaching Methods: There are general rules applicable to these "tell and show" methods that every instructor should know and respect. Let us consider some of them.

Conference:
- Should be used with small groups.
- Requires an able conference leader to control the discussion.
- All participants should contribute to the discussion.
- Develops ability of participants to work with others.
- Useful for exploring different aspects of a problem.
- Participants should be familiar with topic being discussed.
- Requires a relatively great amount of time.
- Time can be wasted by irrelevant discussions.

Training Aids:
- Have aid in place before speech begins.
- Keep aid covered until it is shown to audience.
- Explain aid to audience when it is displayed.
- Display aid so that all can see it.
- Talk to the audience, not to the training aid.
- Use a pointer wherever it is advisable.
- Use assistants as required.
- Aid must be large enough for all to see clearly.
- Cover aid or remove it from view after completing display.
- Do not issue printed material while you are speaking. If you do, the audience will concentrate on the distribution and forget about the speaker. Issue such material before or after the speech.

Note: We have used the term "training aids" which include both the visual and auditory types (printed material, pictures, motion pictures, blackboard, flannel board, charts, graphs, diagrams, exhibits, samples, maps, models, recordings, records, and the like).

Using the Blackboard:
- Make sure you have chalk, colored chalk, and erasers.
- Plan your work in advance.
- If material is complicated, put it on blackboard before speech and cover it until it is required.
- Write and draw clearly; if possible, keep it simple.
- Print and draw so that everyone can see easily.
- Check for glare from different parts of room during rehearsal.
- Use colored chalk for emphasis and clarity.
- Don't crowd material.
- Erase material as soon as it has served its purpose.

Discussions:
   Panel:
   * Presentation by small group of speakers.
   * Questions and discussion by audience follow speeches.
   * Variety of speakers adds interest.
   * Opposing views of speakers stimulate discussion.
   * Care must be exercised to keep discussion on target.
   Forum:
   * Presentation by one speaker.
   * Questions and comments from audience follow presentation.
   * Can involve large number of people in short time.
   * Like all other discussions, it must be controlled.
   Seminar:
   * Group discussion with minimum formal leadership.
   * Participants must be highly experienced with subject.
   * Practical only with small groups.
   * Rules for "conferences" apply to seminars.
   * Especially useful for situations requiring a solution.
   Case Study:
   * Group discussion of a particular case history.
   * Discussion leader must be familiar with case.
   * Brings broad knowledge to bear on individual case.
   * Requires considerable time.
   * Develops skill in analysis and problem-solving.

Demonstrations:
   * Plan carefully how the demonstration will be conducted.

- Prepare a step-by-step outline.
- Rehearse, following outline from start to finish.
- Arrange equipment before actual demonstration.
- Demonstrate only one step at a time.
- Show how and explain how at the same time.
- Use assistants as required.
- Use training aids wherever possible.
- Ask questions of audience to check on understanding.
- Encourage questions from audience.
- Emphasize key points.
- Demonstrate skillfully to set a good example.

Motion Pictures:
- If a good film is available, use it.
- Preview the film and make notes of its content.
- Introduce film to audience; describe content of film and advise audience what to look for.
- Encourage questions after film is shown.
- Where appropriate, conduct discussion concerning the film.
- Caution: Instructors sometimes rely on motion pictures too heavily. The film should not be expected to do the whole job of instruction. Motion pictures should be used as aids or as supplements to the overall training effort.

C. The Summary Part of the Presentation

The introduction opened the presentation stage, the explanation furnished the new material, and now it is up to the summary to conclude the speech on a high note.

Restate, Review, Discuss, Closing Statement: The summary should restate the speech objective, then review the key points in the explanation. Questions should be invited, and any ensuing discussion carefully controlled by the instructor. If no questions are raised by the audience, it is appropriate for the instructor to ask a few questions of the audience. At the proper time, the discussion should be concluded and a strong closing statement should be given. Realize that the last words of a speech are most often the ones remembered by the listeners. Remember also that newspaper reporters (or other persons in the audience who will repeat the theme of your talk) pay a great deal of attention to your closing remarks. For these reasons, you should give extra attention to this phase of your speech. You should choose its content carefully, you should rehearse it thoroughly, then you should deliver it as sincerely and enthusiastically as you possibly can.

We have discussed the introduction, the explanation, and the summary. We have completed the presentation and we now proceed to the application stage.

3.   Application Stage of Instruction (Performance)

We now consider the third stage of instruction. Up to this point, the instructor planned the instruction (first stage), and then told and showed the audience the material involved (second stage); so far, only the eyes and ears of the student have played a dominant role. Now we bring the rest of the students' bodies into the learning process. In the application phase, we apply the knowledge through performance. The students actually get involved; they use their hands, arms, voices, eyes, or whatever other part of the body is required to do the practical exercises involved in the instruction. The points to be considered when conducting practical exercises or role-playing are as follows:

Practical Exercises:
- Since students must perform, they must know exactly what they are required to do.
- Give clear directions to students.
- Make sure students understand why the operation is necessary.
- Set forth the standards of performance.
- Allow sufficient time for students to achieve required standard.
- Supervise performance closely.
- See that students perform correctly.
- Students should master each step before proceeding to the one that follows.
- Repeat explanation and demonstration as the need arises.
- After proper execution is achieved, speed can be developed.
- Students should perform in a realistic setting.
- Students should be encouraged to ask questions.
- Instructor should ask questions to check understanding.
- Instructor should be patient.
- Coach and pupil method may be employed. This will enable advanced students to assist slower students.

Role-Playing:
- Deals with problems which students will meet in future activities.
- Students are given roles to play in simulated situations involving work-related problems.
- Audience observes as each situation is played by different students.
- When a supervisor plays the role of a subordinate, he is required to exercise empathy; to think in terms of the needs of the subordinate.

- When a subordinate plays the role of a supervisor, he is required to exercise empathy; to think in terms of the needs of the supervisor.
- Role-playing requires skillful leadership.
- Especially useful for human relations training.
- Especially helpful in improving attitudes and behavior.

Note: Role-playing can have a tremendous impact on the audience. While training police officers, some of the role-playing situations we portrayed resulted in highly improved patrol performance. In two instances, it was reported to me that the lessons learned from our role-playing were directly responsible for the saving of two lives.

This type of training is not easy to do well. It requires more time in planning, in execution, and in follow-up. However, it is well worth the extra effort. Its content is remembered by the student long after the lessons learned from more conventional types of teaching have been forgotten.

4. Examination Stage of Instruction

This is the fourth stage. By examining the student, the instructor can determine how much has been learned. These results tell the instructor whether he can proceed to new material, or whether he must review what has been taught.

Types of Examinations

There are several types of examinations. Each is used in a different way to achieve its particular purpose. We will consider the observation test, the oral test, the performance test, and the written test.

A. Observation Test: The most informal type of examination, this is especially valuable in measuring those characteristics which do not lend themselves to testing by other means. When we apply an observation test to measure efficiency, attitude, or behavior, it is important that we identify the points to be observed, then apply them uniformly.

Establish Standards for Observation Test: In addition, realistic standards of acceptability must be established. These standards must be made known to each individual being rated. When observation tests are made, the characteristics being tested are measured against required standards in order to evaluate their degree of acceptability.

Danger—Rater's Personal Feelings May Affect Rating: Observation tests are difficult to apply in a uniform manner. The instructor must be careful not to let an opinion or bias influence judgment. Even the mental attitude or physical condition of the rater may unfairly affect the ratings he gives. A rater who feels great at 10 o'clock on a beautiful day might be inclined to give a high rating for a certain level of competence. That same rater who has a headache at 4:30 on a dismal, snowy afternoon might be inclined to give a lower rating for the same level of competence.

Promote Uniformity for Observation Test: Wherever large numbers of students are being rated, an observation test check list should be used to promote uniformity. When observations are made, the rater should not trust his memory to remember the details. These details should be recorded at once and should serve as a basis for entries on the observation test check list.

B. Oral Tests: The oral test serves as an on-the-spot check to determine student understanding. It should be used frequently. A recommended way in which to employ the oral test is for the instructor to ask questions of the students on several occasions during his lecture.

The Construction and Utilization of Questions: Questions should be constructed in conformance with certain guidelines. Questions should be asked in an approved manner. Let us examine the criteria for making questions most effective.

How to construct a question:

- Its content should be clear and unambiguous.
- Its number of words should be kept to a minimum consistent with clarity.
- It must have a specific purpose.
- Only one point should be emphasized.
- It must require a definite answer.
- It should be understood by the student.
- It should be related to the "how" and "why" aspect of the subject matter.
- It should not require a simple "Yes" or "No" answer.
- It should encourage thinking and discourage guessing.
- Where possible, it should emphasize an important principle.

Note: All these points could be applied to *written* questions as well as *oral* questions.

How to Ask an Oral Question:

- Pause, then ask the question. To be most effective, the question should be directed to the entire audience.
- Pause. While pausing, you should search the faces of the audience. If a quizzical look is registered on almost every countenance, this means

you should rephrase the question. On the other hand, if the question is understood, your visual search is almost sure to encounter one individual whose eyes practically plead to be called upon.

- Call on student by name, or
- Call for a volunteer.
- Discuss and evaluate the student's response.

Note: An instructor could also use the rhetorical question. Here he would ask the question, pause, then answer the question himself.

C. *Performance Test:* This test is designed to determine how well a student can perform a specific task. A typing test may require a letter to be typed within a certain time limit. A shooting test may require fifty shots to be fired at a target from five different positions. A speechmaking test may require the delivery of a three-minute talk.

After a student has completed a course, he may be able to pass a written test with an extremely high mark. However, if he is asked to perform, that same student may not be able to put his knowledge into practice. For this reason, whenever a manual skill is involved, a performance test should be administered in order to determine the true capability of the student.

D. *Written Test:* This is the most versatile and the most widely used type of test. Some reasons for its universal popularity follow:

- Has many choices of format such as true-false, multiple-choice, fill-in, essay, limited essay, reading interpretation, among many others.
- Many tests can be rated by machine.
- Has great objectivity; effect of bias and opinion is kept to minimum.

- Simple to administer.
- Large numbers can take the same test in different locations.
- Provides a permanent record of test content and results.
- Provides a basis for discussion between instructor and student.
- Capable of precise marking; to the fraction of a point if necessary.
- Assures uniform content and rating.

Positive Results of Examinations: If a conscientious student knows that he will be required to take an examination, he is going to be ready when the test comes. He will expend extra effort in order to master the material on the examination. This represents a good reason for including the examination stage of instruction.

In addition, the examination can be used to re-emphasize the key points of the instruction. Also, by reviewing the marks achieved by students on the examination, an evaluation of instructional effectiveness can be determined. Also, by analyzing how various subjects on the examination were handled, it is possible to discover weaknesses in the instructional effort and to plan for remedial action.

5. Review Stage of Instruction

This is the fifth and final stage of instruction. At this point, the instructor addresses himself to a review of the key elements of the material taught. By reviewing these elements, the instructor gives them added emphasis, which serves to make a deeper and more lasting impression on the student.

Discussion, Summary, and Closing Statement: Through-out this review, the audience should be encouraged to ask questions or otherwise contribute to the discussion. Since this is the last time the subject is discussed, the instructor should try to make the review as comprehensive and meaningful as possible.

To conclude the review stage, the instructor should summarize the instruction; then make a sincere and enthusiastic closing statement.

nine
Special
Speech
Situations

The majority of speeches seem to follow a "normal pattern." At the outset, an invitation is extended to the speaker. After accepting, he or she usually has several weeks to prepare. The speaker gathers material, makes an outline, rehearses and delivers the speech. This sounds like a pat solution—and it is. We have over-simplified because it is impossible to describe a "normal pattern" that includes all the speech situations you may encounter.

In this chapter we identify and discuss special speech situations. Some of these, like using a microphone, may be present in a great proportion of speeches. Others may be encountered so rarely that a speaker may have to deal with them only once or twice in a speaking career. However, in order to be considered an accomplished speaker, you must be aware of the manner in which to handle the following speech situations.

IMPROMPTU SPEAKING

When you speak from notes—refer to notes on cards or in a speech outline—you speak extemporaneously. When you give an impromptu speech, there are no notes. You are called upon without advance notice, and you must think about what you will say as you rise and while you are on your feet. It is an excellent idea to begin your talk by recognizing appropriate individuals. It is also recommended that you refer to previous speakers. But after that, what do you say?

Impromptu Situation-Saver

On a previous page we talked about situation-savers. We recommended that you be prepared in case a speaking emergency arose. If, in the future, you are unexpectedly called upon to speak, this certainly could be classified as a speaking emergency and you should take steps to be prepared.

Prepare for Impromptu Talk

Your preparation begins when you think ahead. You should anticipate that this will happen to you someday. Now that you have established a need, jot down the titles of several issues you feel are of great importance. Look over the list and pick the one that has importance for the most people beside yourself. Make up a five-minute talk on this subject. Include an introduction, an explanation, and a closing statement. (These three parts of a talk could be paraphrased as: "Tell them what you're going to tell them . . . tell them . . . then tell them what you told them.")

Keep Notes in Your Wallet

A few days after you make this first draft of your talk, you should return to the outline and revise its content. Keep changing it until you are satisfied that it is ready for rehearsal. After the first rehearsal, again make required changes. After you run through a completely satisfactory rehearsal, have your five minute talk typed in outline form. After it is typed, fold it neatly and put it into your wallet. Thereafter, whenever you attend any function at which there is the remotest possibility that you may be called upon to speak, you need only take out your situation-saver speech outline, refresh your memory regarding its content, then hope to be called upon so you can give an inspired "impromptu" speech based upon the notes in your wallet.

If Prepared Notes Are Inappropriate

It may be possible that the notes you have prepared are inappropriate and cannot be used. In such a case, your pre-planning will still help. Because you have anticipated the possibility of being called upon, you will find yourself seeking alternatives in case your speech can't be used. You will be making notes of names, of previous speaker's remarks, of any items you can use in an impromptu speech situation.

By making preparation, you acquire confidence. This attitude promotes an easy flow of words. You find yourself enriching your brief talk with facts, illustrations, and examples that have meaning for the audience you are addressing.

Be Brief

The impromptu talk should be brief. After you have given your message to the audience, make a strong closing statement, and sit down.

HOW TO INTRODUCE A SPEAKER

When you are given the task of introducing a speaker, the first thing to do is to get information that will help you carry out your assignment. Ascertain how he likes his name to be pronounced. Ask him about his education, family, work, hobbies, membership in organizations, and any other area you deem to be of interest to the audience. Make notes of all the items you plan to include in your introduction. At the bottom of these items, print the name of the speaker in LARGE letters. Do not trust your memory with this most important part of the entire introduction. On one of his TV shows, Merv Griffin depended on his memory and referred to Tony Martin as Tony Bennett.

Content of Introduction

In your introduction, you should tell the audience why they should listen. Let them know how they will benefit. In order to increase audience receptivity, the listeners should be advised of the speaker's credentials which qualify him to speak on the subject.

Delivering the Introduction

Your introduction should be brief, just a minute or two. It should not be memorized. It should be concluded by announcing the speaker's name clearly and correctly.

After the introduction, you should leave the platform immediately. If you have done your job well, the speaker will get off to a good start as soon as the applause you have generated subsides.

RHETORICAL QUESTIONS

The rhetorical question is not asked in order to obtain an answer from the audience. Rather, its purpose is to arouse interest and to stimulate thought concerning the issue under consideration. For example, if I were giving a talk to encourage people to ride bicycles, I might open the talk with this series of rhetorical questions. "Do you want to live longer? Do you want a hobby that the whole family can enjoy? Do you want to save money? Do you want to conserve gasoline?"

Follow-Up on Rhetorical Questions

After asking these questions with a substantial pause after each one, the audience has its interest aroused. The speaker then develops each question into a major part of the speech. By answering the questions, the speaker strives to sell the audience on riding bicycles.

HOW TO USE THE MICROPHONE

During your rehearsal, you should decide whether you will or will not use a microphone. Once you have decided to use it, become fully acquainted with the way it operates. Check the controls so you will be able to regulate the volume if the need arises. If an extension cord is used, find out the location of the wall fixture into which it is plugged. This knowledge proves valuable in the event that the sound amplification system suddenly becomes inoperative because some individual accidentally caused a disconnection with his feet or chair.

Rehearsing with Microphone

During the rehearsal, use the microphone in exactly the same way that you will during the actual speech. Ordinarily, the microphone should be a little less than an arm's length away from your mouth. Do not crowd the microphone or speak directly into it. You should position the microphone so it is a little below the height of your shoulders. This position enables you to speak over the microphone as you maintain eye contact with your audience.

Movements with a Fixed Microphone

Even though you are using a fixed microphone, it is possible for you to shift your position slightly. Ordinarily you face the center of the audience and speak over the microphone. Occasionally, you can move slightly to either side of the microphone to address your remarks to someone on the left or right side of the audience. This can be done effectively if you maintain the same distance from the microphone and you still speak directly over it.

Movements with a Lapel Microphone

Wherever possible, you should ask for a lapel microphone. Once you have attached this microphone to your clothing, you don't have to worry about keeping the microphone in the proper spot between you and the audience. The lapel microphone permits you to move anywhere on the platform. However, a word of caution is in order. You must be aware that a wire is trailing behind you. When you reverse your direction, your feet may become entangled in the wire. After a few rehearsals with a lapel microphone, you will master the art of controlling the trailing wire.

Changing the Volume of the Voice

When using the microphone, you should continue to speak in a conversational tone. If you want to emphasize a point by changing your volume, move a little farther away when you raise your voice and a bit closer when you lower it. Do not touch the microphone when you are speaking. You may damage the instrument or cause a distracting feedback.

Preparation in Lieu of Rehearsal

If you are one of a series of speakers and you have had no opportunity to rehearse with the microphone, there is something you can do to prepare for your appearance. Note carefully how each of the speakers who precede you adjust the microphone and how they utilize it. Note the most effective technique, then adopt a similar procedure when your turn comes to speak.

ANSWERING QUESTIONS

When you are asked a question by someone in the audience, you should make sure you understand it before attempting to answer it. To best accomplish this, you should repeat the question. If the individual agrees that

your restatement is correct, you can proceed with your
answer.

Other Benefits from Repeating the Question

When you repeat the question, in addition to getting a
clear idea of the question content, other benefits are
realized. The entire audience is made aware of the content
of the question. In almost every case, when a person asks
a question, he employs a level of volume just about sufficient to reach the speaker's ears. As a result, the audience
has no idea what was asked. If the speaker proceeds to
answer the question without repeating it, the audience
is in the dark, and most of the value of the question is lost.

Benefit to Speaker

Another benefit of repeating the question is realized by
the speaker. This repetition gives him additional time to
decide how he will handle the question. If he chooses to
answer the question himself, he has more time to formulate an answer.

For additional information on questions, please refer
to our discussion of this subject under "Helps."

READING A SPEECH

We have indicated that you should never deliver a speech
by reading it unless such a delivery is imperative. If there
is no alternative and you must read the speech, certain
guidelines should be used.

How to Make Reading a Speech Less Dull

The material being read should be held at about shoulder height. This position insures that the reader's voice is projected toward the audience rather than downward toward the floor. The reader should use eye contact when he looks at the audience. He should read ahead to the end of a sentence, then look at an individual and give him the closing words of the thought contained by the sentence. At the end of each sentence, the reader should pause slightly as he drops his eyes to the manuscript to continue reading. This slight pause following each eye contact with the audience adds to the effectiveness of the reading since it makes the reading more natural.

Practice

Good reading is achieved only through practice. As you rehearse, strive to make the reading sound like a conversation. Try to read as if you were speaking from notes. Make sure you exhibit sincerity and enthusiasm as well as other desirable speech techniques.

PUBLIC RELATIONS SPEECH

Any organization can derive a tremendous benefit if its representatives who are in contact with the public make a favorable impression. Instead of analyzing the public relations speech by setting forth a list of "do's and don'ts," we will use an illustration. We will examine the delivery of an extremely effective speech of this type.

The Setting

Out in Colorado, about a half hour's ride from Denver, is the Red Rocks Theatre. This is a natural amphitheatre into which a stage and seating for thousands of spectators were installed. Every summer season, various types of entertainment are presented there.

My Attendance

I attended this outdoor spectacle twice. On both occasions I was impressed by the musical artists who performed. Judging by the applause, everyone in the audience seemed similarly affected by the outstanding entertainment.

My Surprise

What surprised me most on each of my two visits was the fact that the loudest and most enthusiastic applause was accorded to an individual who was not a musician, singer, dancer, or any other type of entertainer. This individual who evoked the warmest response from the audience was a police officer. Strange as it seems, and as hard as it is to believe, a police officer in uniform walked on the stage, spoke for less than five minutes, then left the stage—as the red rocks forming the walls of the theatre echoed to the applause of practically every person in the audience. How did he do it?

The Police Officer Greets the Audience

In Colorado, in the summer, the sun sets after the performance begins at the Red Rocks Theatre. By the time the intermission comes, night has fallen and the surrounding hills are in complete darkness. Just before the entertainment resumes after the last intermission, a police officer steps out on the stage, walks to the microphone and says warmly, "Good evening ladies and gentlemen . . . I hope you are enjoying the show!"

The Speech

The officer stands smiling as the audience responds to his opening remark. When all is quiet he says to the thousands of spectators:

> When you came here this evening, it was daylight. After you parked your car, you had no trouble walking to this theatre and finding your seat. Now it is dark. Unless we do a little planning, you may not be able to find your car.
>
> To begin with, please remember how you approached the entrance to this theatre. Did you come down the hill, or up the hill? If you can't remember, please come to the stage after the performance and I will help you.
>
> For those who remember how they approached the entrance, please reverse the procedure when you leave here. If you walked down, go up; if you walked up, go down. Now you are on the right path but you must find the lot where your car is parked. To do this, please look at the stub which the parking attendant gave to you. Notice the large letter on the stub. On your walk away from here, when you come to that letter, enter that parking lot. Now look at the number on your stub after the letter. When you walk to that number you should find your car. If you run into problems in the parking lot, look for an attendant and he will help you. If you lost your stub, come to the stage after the performance and I will help you.
>
> When you drove here this evening, all of the roads had two-way traffic. Vehicles were leaving and vehicles were arriving. As you recall, the roads were jammed and traffic moved slowly. When you leave here, there will be no in-

coming vehicles and all traffic will be moving out from the parking lots. For this reason, all the roads will have one-way traffic in your direction.

If you run into problems with your car, drive off the road and keep your lights on. Our emergency patrol car will come to your assistance.

We hope you get home safely. Please enjoy the rest of the show.

Why the Audience Applauded Loudly

It is not difficult to understand why the audience applauded this speech so enthusiastically. The officer anticipated a problem which the audience might meet and he provided a solution. In other words, he practiced empathy; throughout the talk, he spoke in terms of his listener's interests. Every sentence was concerned with the welfare of his audience.

One Speaker Impresses Hundreds of Thousands of Listeners

There must have been more than five thousand persons in that audience. If you multiply this number by the number of performances, you will realize that this one police officer made a favorable impression on several hundred thousand people in a single summer season. More importantly, he reflected credit on the entire police profession.

PRESENTATION SPEECH

The purpose of the presentation speech is to honor someone. The first thing the speaker must do is to get background material.

The Recipient, the Accomplishment, the Award, and the Sponsor

Regarding the recipient, the speaker should obtain facts about his education, work, family, and the like. Regarding the recipient's accomplishment, the speaker should find out the when, where, who, what, how, and why concerning it. If an award is to be presented, the speaker should obtain information concerning its history and the organization behind the award.

Brevity

The speech of presentation should be brief; however, it should contain sufficient details to provide deserving praise for the recipient, for his accomplishment, and for the sponsor of the award.

Accuracy

It is important that all the names, dates, and other factual information are stated correctly. For this reason, your speech of presentation should be given from notes. Even though it is a short speech, to trust your memory is to court disaster and embarrassment.

EULOGY

The eulogy resembles the speech of presentation in several ways. Both honor someone. Both require research. Both should be delivered from notes. Both should have accurate details.

Delivery of the Eulogy

However, the eulogy also differs from the speech of presentation in several ways. The presentation speech is given on a happy note while the eulogy is part of a somber occasion. The speaker at a presentation is rarely in possession of all the information he requires for his talk. The speaker who delivers a eulogy is usually well-acquainted with the deceased. An important part of preparing the eulogy is to select several of the most significant aspects in the life of the deceased and then arrange them in a meaningful manner.

The speech of presentation should be brief but the length of the eulogy varies. In some instances, a short talk would be deemed appropriate. In other circumstances, a lengthy eulogy would be considered proper to pay adequate homage to a certain individual's memory.

NOMINATING SPEECH

In the nominating speech we introduce someone, then we make statements regarding his qualifications for the office he seeks. All the rules set forth on previous pages regarding the introduction of an individual to an audience apply to the nominating speech.

The Office and the Candidate

In addition, we should identify the requirements of the office or position being sought. After acquainting the audience with the office, we should show how our candidate fulfills each requirement.

Character of the Nominating Speech

The nominating speech should be brief. It should be specific, and the use of generalizations avoided. The information in the speech must be accurate. The closing statement should be a sincere and enthusiastic nomination of the candidate.

ACCEPTANCE SPEECH

The acceptance speech could follow the announcement of a nomination or an award. We will consider what both types have in common, then we will discuss each one separately.

General Attributes of Acceptance Speeches

Acceptance speeches for both award and nomination require the recipient to express his appreciation. The individual or organization responsible for making it happen should be identified and thanked. Both speeches should be as brief as possible. They should be sincere. Humor should be used only if the person who made the award or nomination set a humorous tone with his or her speech. Give credit to others; don't make it appear as though you earned this honor all by yourself. Mention your plans for the future to show you intend to keep up the good work.

Nomination Acceptance Speech

Upon accepting a nomination, the recipient must give the impression that he is eager and capable of conducting a vigorous campaign. He must remember that he is part of an organization, and should refer to the team effort needed to win the election.

Award Acceptance Speech

Upon receiving an award, accept it with your left hand so that your right hand is free to grasp the hand of the donor. If the award is very large, put it down while you make your speech. Even though your acceptance speech is short, make sure that you rehearse it so you begin and end on a high note.

SPEAKING AT A NEWS CONFERENCE

When newspaper reporters attend a news conference, they are looking for a story. The more sensational the content, the better they like it. Make sure that you do not inadvertently say something which could be innocently misinterpreted or, as may happen, could be *intentionally* misinterpreted by some over-zealous headline-seeker.

In 1977, I was the Chairman of the United States Tennis Open at Forest Hills. I was asked to speak at a news conference. This came as a surprise and I had no time to prepare. My impromptu talk covered several different items. One reporter misconstrued my remarks and asked for a clarification, which I promptly provided. Next day, several newspapers carried headlines on their sport pages reflecting a misinterpretation of my speech. Why had the reporters done this? Because the true meaning of all my remarks did not make news, but a mis-quote, based upon incomplete facts, provided an attention-getting headline.

If, at some time in the future, you are required to speak at a news conference, prepare carefully. Your speech should be typewritten word for word. Copies should be available for each member of the press who is present and for transmission to those news services and newspapers which are not in attendance.

In a situation like this, it would be forgivable if you read your speech from your prepared script. If, however, you want to make it more enjoyable for your listeners and you decide to speak from notes, you should exercise precautions. Your notes should be more detailed than usual. You should rehearse more completely. At least one rehearsal should include a listener whose sole purpose is to act the part of a "devil's advocate." This critical listener should play the role of a reporter intent on finding hidden meanings in your remarks.

On an earlier page, we observed that there were four possible versions of a speech: the one you prepared, the one you gave, the one you wished you had given while on your way home, and the one that the press says that you gave. At a news conference, several reporters will be ready to hear your speech and then report on what you said. To heighten the possibility of obtaining the press reaction you want, make sure your words accurately reflect your notes.

SPEAKING ON RADIO

Some years ago, I was asked if I would consent to be interviewed on radio. After agreeing to do so, I appeared at the studio at the designated time. After a short con-

versation with the announcer we proceeded to a sound-
proof booth. The announcer stated that he was going to
ask me questions regarding my school activities. He
urged me to be natural. He said that I should answer his
questions in whatever way I saw fit. He wanted our talk
to seem like an ordinary, everyday conversation.

Taping the Interview

The announcer turned on a tape recorder, put a few introductory remarks on the tape, then asked me the first
question. We chatted in a question-and-answer format
for about ten minutes. At the end of our conversation,
the announcer made a few closing remarks and turned
off the recorder. A few minutes later, I left the studio.

Follow Directions and Be Natural

If you are invited to speak on the radio, accept. Your
experience will probably be very similar to mine. Just
follow directions and act natural and you will perform
effectively.

Delivering a Speech on Radio

There is a rare possibility that you will be asked to make
a speech on radio. If this occurs, begin your preparation
for it exactly the way you would if you were scheduled
to go before a live audience. During your rehearsal and
the delivery of your talk in the studio, one thing will be
very different—you will have no support from your audience. To make up for this missing inspiration, you have
to exercise a little imagination. In order to stimulate
your sincerity and enthusiasm, you should imagine that
you are before a live audience. Pick out some object, like
a picture or a plant, across the room and imagine that it

is a face. Then deliver your speech to that imagined face as though it was telling you that you were doing a wonderful job. Do this and your voice will sound animated, interesting, and pleasant to those who listen to you on the radio.

Delayed, But Pleasant, Audience Response

No matter what form your radio appearance takes, be prepared for a satisfying after-effect. For days following your radio performance, your friends will be telling you how much they enjoyed your remarks.

TELEVISION APPEARANCES

During the Vietnam War, the United States Army directed the Civil Affairs Branch to prepare a fifteen-minute television program. This program had to reflect the activities of Civil Affairs. It was to be shown with similar programs from other branches to spell out the manner in which the Army discharges the overall responsibilities of its mission.

Major McCullough Assigned

Because I had previous experience with television, I was given the assignment of preparing the script, designing and procuring the necessary art work and exhibits, and going before the television camera to do a solo job of narrating the entire show.

Preliminary Planning

We had a deadline to meet, so there was no time to lose. We visited the library and researched texts and manuals. We gathered material relating to all the activities of Civil

Affairs. We then prepared an outline of a script, and we determined what art work and exhibits were necessary. After leaving an order with the Training Aids Division for the drawings and other items, we sat down to write the script.

The Script

A speech to an audience is given from notes, but a television speech is based on a script that must be followed closely. This is so because of the time factor and because the cameraman must know exactly when he must shift from the speaker to an exhibit then back to the speaker.

Conferences, Rehearsals, Taping

After the script and art work were complete, we conferred with the engineers, technicians, and cameramen at the Signal Corps. We constructed the set and set a date for rehearsal. During the rehearsals, several changes were needed. When these changes were accomplished, a satisfactory rehearsal was achieved. We then moved to the actual "takes." On the fourth try, the director was satisfied and the tape was ready for showing to a television audience.

If You Must Produce a Television Show . . .

That you will have to produce a television show as we did is unlikely. However, if you ever get such an assignment, apply yourself to the task and you will be amazed at how well you perform. As I did, you will find that people are willing to help if you approach them with politeness and respect.

Discussion Show on Television

Though you may never do your own TV show, it is quite possible that you may be asked someday to appear on television. If you are part of a discussion show, prepare by reading material relating to the subject to be discussed. Try to obtain information on its latest programs, statistics, legislation, or other developments that affect the subject. When you appear at the studio, follow carefully the advice given. When the program commences, give your full attention to the moderator, the person who is running the show before the camera. By concentrating on him or her, you forget that you are "on camera." When this happens, you are more natural and more effective.

Speech on Television

If you are invited to make a speech on television, you should prepare your notes just as you would for a normal speaking effort. During your rehearsal, pick out an object on the opposite wall and imagine it is the camera. Just as we did with the radio speech, go a step further and imagine that the camera is the face of an individual to whom you are speaking. This will produce two benefits during your television speech: first, it will get you to look at the camera, which will give the viewers at home the impression that you are looking at them; second, by imagining that the camera is a friendly face, you may derive inspiration from this inanimate object in much the same way as an artist does from a beautiful sunrise or sunset.

A Ninety-Year-Old who Epitomizes Sincerity and Enthusiasm

When Arthur Rubinstein celebrated his ninetieth birthday, I was greatly impressed by the sincerity and enthusiasm he generated. I watched him play Grieg's Piano Concerto in A Minor. His facial expressions were something to behold. Each one seemed to mirror the emotions created within his body by the beauty of the music.

After his performance, Mr. Rubinstein was interviewed. During the interview he said that the true artist must "sing inside" as he is doing the thing he loves. He said that he cannot play the piano and communicate with the audience as does the average performer. He is therefore required to give his message through facial expressions. As the audience looks at Rubinstein's face, they sense that he is being carried away by the music and they cannot help but experience a similar emotion. Mr. Rubinstein describes it as "a certain antenna from my emotion, or if you like, my soul." Just as Arthur Rubinstein concentrates on his piano and music to the exclusion of all else, so you should concentrate on your notes and the camera. By following this technique, your antenna will reach your audience and they will be deeply impressed by your sincerity and enthusiasm.

Prompter Cards

When I made my television program, I used prompter cards which provided me with the cues for a natural delivery of my talk. When you rehearse at home or at work, make several cards containing the key words of your talk. Have someone display these cards next to the object you have chosen as your imagined camera/face. While concentrating on the object, permit your peripheral vision to pick up the word for your next thought. While you are developing and completing this thought, your assistant displays the next card which your peripheral vision picks up at the appropriate time. By practicing this technique, you appear natural as you deliver your talk.

Your Attitude and Action Before the Camera

Practice stands you in good stead in the television studio. The prompting devices they may provide are more sophisticated and easier to use. In the studio, listen carefully to the instructions given. When you take your place in front of the camera, awaiting your signal to start speaking, you feel very lonely. At that moment your rehearsals pay off. When you look at that camera and imagine it is a friendly face giving you support, you are on familiar ground and you are in a prime position to put forth an inspired effort with an abundant display of sincerity and enthusiasm.

MOTION PICTURE APPEARANCES

Some years ago I received a contract to write and participate in a half-hour training film depicting the proper way to testify in court. We called it *On the Witness Stand.* In the film, a police officer named "Chesty Novice" does everything wrong and is soundly rebuked by the judge. After some appropriate remarks by a narrator, into the courtroom comes "Chester No-vice" who does everything correctly. Throughout the film there were cuts to the narrator who provided a running account, along with an explanation of what was taking place.

Motion Picture Scripts

As mentioned when we discussed the script for television, the motion picture script differs greatly from the notes used in delivering the average speech. The motion picture script contains a word-for-word account of what is to be said. In addition, a shooting script describes each scene by number and the type of camera shot to be used. Notations appear concerning the scene, the props, and the positions of the characters. Before each scene is put on film, there are lengthy conferences involving the director, the lighting technicians, sound technicians, and cameramen.

Lights, Camera, Action

If you are scheduled to appear in a motion picture, be prepared for long waits between appearances before the camera. Then, when you are scheduled to appear, be prepared to perform exactly the way the director wants you to perform. It seems as though the average director feels that the actor is only one more of his many headaches, and he can't be expected to tolerate mistakes. In other words, when the actor comes before the camera he is supposed to do things right, not wrong. If you do things right, the expense of salaries, lights, film, equipment, rentals, and the like, all come to an end. If you do things wrong, they can double or triple. In an atmosphere like this, it is understandable that you, the actor, feel pressure. You also can understand why people in show business get ulcers.

The Answer to Pressure

What is the answer? We provided the solution where we discussed preparation, rehearsal, and nervousness. If you prepare properly and rehearse until your performance is near perfection, you are ready. When you come before the cameras, if you are normal and you want to do a good job, you must be nervous. Realizing this, you accept nervousness and make it work for you. You determine to love your audience (the camera) and give an Academy Award performance. By engaging in positive action and by adopting a positive attitude, your confidence grows and your performance becomes more effective.

STAGE APPEARANCES

During a one-year period in my career, I wrote thirty playlets ranging in length from three to thirty minutes. These playlets depicted activities performed by police officers during their normal course of duty.

Background of Playlet Program

These playlets were presented in a theatre at 23rd St. and Lexington Avenue in New York City. Of the cast of twelve in our troupe, three of the actors handled the principal roles and they appeared in all the playlets over a five-year period. Nine of the actors were chosen from the class to which the thirty playlets were being presented. In addition, we had a curtain manager (responsible for the movements of three curtains), a lighting manager, a prop manager, and a script manager. We performed five playlets each Wednesday afternoon. I served as producer, director, and narrator.

The Production Schedule

Every Thursday, the roles for the next week's performance were assigned. All the players sat in a circle and we read our lines. The players took their scripts home to study their lines. On Monday we had a walk-through rehearsal.

On Tuesday came the dress rehearsal in preparation for the next day's performance.

The Performance

Our audiences ranged from several hundred to two thousand. Each week there was the anticipation and excitement of a new production for a new audience. When the audience was seated, the house lights dimmed and the narrator introduced the playlet. At the proper moment the curtain opened and the actors occupied the spotlight.

Scope of Presentations

Although all of our performers were amateurs, our "Academy Playhouse" took on a professional air after our first year of working together. To give some idea of the scope of our presentations, our props included an automobile which was rolled onstage as required. Our "Public Relations" playlet, which ran for almost a half-hour, was composed of sixteen different vignettes. In the first four, Police Officer Snafu mishandled four problems brought to him by four different civilians. He acted rudely and the citizen's feelings were hurt. In the second four vignettes, each of the civilians is involved with a situation affecting the police department. They remember Snafu and respond angrily; the consequences of their actions prove to be detrimental to the interests of the police. In the next four vignettes, Always Everready is faced with the same four problems brought to him by the same civilians who appeared in the first episodes. Everready performs in a commendable manner and the citizens express their gratitude. The last four vignettes show the civilians responding warmly and going out of their way to cooperate and help a police department which includes men like their benefactor, Officer Always Everready. One of our stars became so skillful that he resigned from the Police Department, went to Hollywood, and subsequently appeared in leading roles in several television productions.

Our Experience with Stage Performers

During our five-year run in New York City, we schooled and directed over one hundred male and female performers. Never did we encounter a neophyte actor who asked to be excused because he could not handle his stage appearances. We insisted that the actors prepare thoroughly, we rehearsed faithfully, and we performed every playlet with sincerity and enthusiasm.

Our Advice to the Players

If you are ever faced with a stage appearance, prepare thoroughly, rehearse faithfully and perform with sincerity and enthusiasm. Chances are that your stage appearance will be one of the most exciting and memorable events of your entire speaking career.

THE LIVELY SPEECH

There is nothing more boring than a dull speech. If a speech is dull, it is the fault of the speaker. If the speaker takes the trouble to investigate why his speech is bad, he will find that the trouble began with his preparation.

Avoid the Cut-and-Dried Lecture

At the outset, a speaker should determine to present something a bit different—something that arouses interest and maintains attention. Instead of offering a cut-and-dried lecture, he should consider the use of a panel, conference, forum, debate, case study, seminar, or recordings and playbacks. He or she can show pictures, motion pictures, charts, diagrams, exhibits, demonstrations, or skits. The speaker can conduct role playing, quiz contests, practical exercises, or performance tests. He or she (or you) can do many things to make any presentation come alive.

Your Delivery Will Sparkle

Dare to be different and you will have an appreciative audience. Of course it is a little more work, but it is worth it. If your speech sparkles because of original thinking, then your delivery sparkles. You find that you enjoy presenting material which arouses the interest and maintains the attention of your audience.

LEADING A DISCUSSION

Wherever you find a conference, a forum, a panel, or any other type of discussion, you will find a moderator keeping the comments of the participants on the right course. If the moderator fails to do his job, the discussion strays and produces few, if any, results. If the moderator does his job well, the discussion focuses on the problem under consideration, and the objective of the panel, forum, or conference is achieved.

What It Takes to Be a Moderator

Serving as a moderator is more difficult than being an effective speaker, because the moderator must excel in several areas. In addition to being able to speak extemporaneously; he must be able to talk in an impromptu manner; he must be able to deal with the personalities of the other participants; he must have a broad grasp of the subject under consideration; he must be skilled in controlling the discussion if it threatens to get out of hand and to stimulate it if it begins to wane. The moderator must act as the liaison between the audience and the panelists. He must act as the coordinator among various forces at a conference. From this description, it is apparent that the leader of a discussion must be skilled in many areas. Only a person with such capabilities should attempt to discharge the responsibilities of a moderator.

ACCORDION SPEECH

When the New York City Transit Police Academy conducted its first graduation ceremony, I was one of the scheduled speakers. Chief Thomas O'Rourke confided to me that he hoped the three scheduled speeches wouldn't last more than thirty minutes. Since he had no idea how long the other two speakers would talk, he asked if I would do him a favor. Since we were friends, I assured him that I would. He said that he was scheduling me to speak last. If the others spoke for long periods, he asked me to be brief. If the others spoke briefly, he asked me to fill the half-hour.

How the Accordion Speech Was Arranged

Having prepared well and having rehearsed diligently, I was sure that I could tailor my material for a short talk or a long speech. I borrowed a red pencil and went to work on my notes. I circled in red all the most important material to be used for a three-minute talk. I underlined in red the material to be used for a ten-minute talk. With

all my material, I would have no trouble talking for
twenty-five minutes if that proved necessary.

Will the "Accordion" Be Stretched or Compressed?

Chief O'Rourke introduced the representative from the
Federal Bureau of Investigation who drew a paper from
his pocket and read a message from Director J. Edgar
Hoover. He then sat down. Elapsed time: two minutes
and forty-five seconds.

Chief O'Rourke introduced the Chairman of the New
York City Board of Transportation who extended his
greetings and best wishes. He then sat down. Elapsed
time: two minutes flat.

Chief O'Rourke then introduced his "accordionist"
who spoke for the rest of the half-hour.

The Last Shall Be First

According to the graduation programs, I actually had
third billing behind the other two speakers. However,
when the ceremony was over, the pictures taken and the
stories written concerned my presentation. Next day in
Miami, Florida, a friend of mine named Frank Mascola
purchased a *New York Times* which carried the story
of my speech.

Prepare Well and You Can Adjust the Speech Well

Only sound preparation and rehearsal permitted me to
shorten or lengthen my talk like an accordion. Only sincerity and enthusiasm made those camera shutters click
and made those reporters write up their accounts of my
speech.

In the future, if you are faced with such a speech situation, have no qualms. As long as you have prepared well, you can tailor the speech to fit your needs.

HOW THE SPEAKER CAN USE A RECORDING MACHINE

The recording machine can make a real contribution to your speaking career: in the classroom, to the neophyte speaker, for rehearsals, to detect speech flaws, to make a permanent record of talks, to record conferences, as an accompaniment for slides or films, or for use in effective speaking courses.

The Recorder in the Classroom

At St. Lawrence University, the Moran Institute featured classes by more than thirty distinguished lecturers. The class, which generated more interest and discussion than any other, was conducted by Doctor Louis Yablonsky, a sociologist. Lou had worked closely with the youth gangs on the West Side of New York City. He had won the confidence of many gang members and had conducted extensive conferences dealing with their activities. These conferences were recorded on tape.

How Recordings Were Used

These recordings represented the core of Lou's classes. He gave a few introductory remarks, then played a five- or ten-minute tape. Lou then posed a question based on the recording and a spirited discussion ensued. When the subject was sufficiently examined, Lou played another short tape and led another discussion.

Advantages of Using Recordings

These recordings gave life to Lou's classes. To add to their value and practicality, the tapes were extremely easy to store and transport. When Lou arrived on campus, he visited the audio/visual department and arranged for the loan of a machine for playing the tapes. Another advantage was that Lou did not have to carry any notes into the classroom. On the tape container, each different recording was identified and described. These notations were all Dr. Yablonsky needed for the delivery of his introductory remarks. From that point on, the recordings took over, Manhattan's West Side was brought into the classroom, and a deep learning experience followed.

HOW A RECORDER CAN HELP THE INEXPERIENCED SPEAKER

A recording machine can provide a real service for the beginner in the field of effective speaking. With such a piece of equipment and a textbook like this one to guide him, he can make real progress. In addition, if he performs in front of a full-length mirror, the visual sense also becomes involved in the learning process.

The Subject and the Outline

We are going to assume that you have a recorder and you want to get to work. The first step is to select a subject close to your heart that you feel strongly about. Make an outline of a talk dealing with such a subject as follows:

Introduction
1. Background (to get on common ground with audience).
2. Objective (of speech).
3. Motivation (to arouse desire of audience to accept objective).

Explanation
1. Main Point
   A. Support of 1
2. Main Point
   A. Support of 2
   B. Support of 2
      (1) Support of B

Closing Statement
1. Restate objective.
2. Ask for action.

The Outline: What Is Optional and What Is Necessary?

You must realize that the outline shown above is only a sample. You should follow such a format, but every speech outline you ever make will vary as to content. One outline may have only one main point in the explanation and many supporting statements. Another outline may have many main points and few supporting statements. However, all your outlines should have an introduction, explanation, and closing statement.

The Outline: Reading It and Speaking From It

Your speech should take about three minutes. After you have the outline completed, read it aloud exactly as it appears on the paper. After that, prepare to give the speech for the first time while you are seated with the outline in front of you. Mark down the exact time and start your speech. Very likely, you will feel awkward and ill at ease as you formulate your speech from notes for the first time. This is perfectly normal, so don't be concerned. When you finish, jot down the time and figure how long you spoke.

Revising the Outline

Go back over your outline immediately after this first speech you made from its content. Make any changes required as the result of giving your talk. When you finish, get up, stretch, and take a little breather.

Repeat the Speech

After a few minutes, sit down, make a note of the time, and give your speech again. You will probably be amazed to see how much better you do with your second effort.

Record the Speech

Now that you have built up a little confidence, you are ready for your first recording. Turn on the machine and ascertain that it is properly set. In a seated position, get the microphone and your outline in front of you. Jot down the time, press the RECORD switch and begin your speech.

Listen to Your Speech

When you finish, play back your talk. If you have never heard your voice on a tape before, be ready for a surprise. The voice you hear when you speak and the voice your listeners hear are quite different. As you listen to yourself delivering your speech, turn to the "Checklist" at the back of this book. Evaluate your speech in terms of the *musts, helps,* and *avoids.* If you notice serious speaking faults, don't panic. Resolve to correct them, and in time you will.

Stand Up and Give the Speech

Until now, you have performed while seated at a desk or table. Since most speakers deliver their talks from a standing position, that is the next step in the rehearsal process. Set up your microphone at the required height, position your outline, note the time, press the RECORD switch and begin your speech.

Listen to the "Standing Version"

As you play back your "standing version," you should notice a marked improvement in your sincerity and enthusiasm. While seated, you were rather comfortable and relaxed and your voice was not affected by the actions of your body. However, in a standing position you are more inclined to use your hands, arms, and other parts of your body for gestures. This activity is reflected in your voice, making it more animated.

Give the Speech Before a Mirror

If you have a full-length mirror in your home, this can provide another dimension for your rehearsal activity. Set up your speech equipment in front of the mirror so that you can make eye contact with yourself. When you play back this recording, the presence of the mirror should add more color to your voice.

Give the Speech Before an Audience

Best of all, if you can get a live audience for a few of your rehearsals, this adds the finishing touch. If they laugh or applaud at the appropriate time, they will also enjoy hearing their contribution during the playback of the tape.

Important Note

What we have said about rehearsing *with* a recording machine is equally applicable to rehearsals *without* such equipment. Whether with or without a recording machine, whenever you prepare for a speech you must select your subject and make an outline. After this is done, it is helpful if you read your outline aloud, deliver your speech from the outline while seated, deliver the speech while standing, deliver the speech before a mirror, and finally deliver it before an audience.

Also, it should be realized that the use of a recorder for rehearsals is not restricted to the beginner. As you progress and become more experienced, you should continue to consider the use of a recording machine for rehearsals. Any device that will improve the actual speech should be employed by the effective speaker.

RECORDING TAPES
FOR PERMANENT RECORDS

When the average person gives a speech, its content is usually unobtainable a short time after. If the speech was bad, this is a blessing. If the speech was good, this is a tragedy.

Your Creation Deserves to Be Taped

After you work hard doing research for a speech, after you sweat over the content and organization of your outline, after you rehearse and rehearse, the least you can do is make a record of your creation.

Value of Permanent Record

Such a record is invaluable in the event that a need for the same speech arises at some time in the future. In addition, it permits you to measure your progress as a speaker.

Comments can be added on the tape at the conclusion of the speech regarding the effectiveness of demonstrations, charts, exhibits, or any other training aid used during the speech. This serves as a stimulus to repeat the use of such techniques and to experiment with the adoption of other novel approaches.

If you are part of a large organization, tapes from many speakers can be brought together in the library and made available for listening by interested persons.

Recording Conferences

No matter how expert the moderator, much of the benefit of a conference is lost unless preparations are made to capture all the pearls of wisdom that fall from the lips of the participants. The best way to keep a record is by means of a recording machine. After the conference is over, the tape can be replayed and the highlights of its content can be reduced to writing. Copies can then be sent to all participants and other interested individuals for their edification.

Ideal for Brainstorming Session

The recorder is especially valuable in the brainstorming type of conference. Here, the participants are presented with a problem. They are then encouraged to call out solutions as rapidly as possible. It doesn't matter how ridiculous the solution is, as long as ideas keep coming. At a conference like this, only a recording machine can ensure that no good suggestions were lost.

Because a recording machine produces an accurate record, its conference tape can be used to settle any disputes that arise concerning who said what. If so desired, the tape can be identified and explained with a descriptive label and used as a permanent record.

A TAPED NARRATION FOR SLIDES
OR PICTURES

If you are showing a series of slides or pictures, you have three options regarding accompanying sound. You can show them and say nothing. You can describe them as you show them. You can make a taped narration beforehand and synchronize the display of the slides or pictures with the words of the tape.

Narration on Tape Is Generally Best

We favor the third option. The use of a recorded tape provides a professional touch to the presentation. In addition, it frees the speaker for concentration on one thing—the showing of the slides or films.

Coordination and Control Are Essential

Regarding a speech technique like this, close coordination and control are mandatory. Several rehearsals should be conducted to be sure that the slides or pictures are shown at the proper time. On the reel of the tape should be a listing of the order in which the slides or pictures are discussed on the tape. During the final check before the speech, the listing on the tape and the order of pictures or slides in the projector should be checked to see that they match properly.

USING A RECORDER IN AN EFFECTIVE SPEAKING COURSE

The heart of an effective speaking course is the short talks given by the students. Before each class the student prepares the talk, delivers it, hears the instructor comment on his effort, and, finally, hears classmates say how they liked it. However, the speaker still is not sure how he *actually* sounded.

Let the Student Hear What Others Heard

This doubt can be removed with the use of a recording machine. If it is turned on at the beginning of the session and it runs until the end, all the activity can be captured on tape. A special session can then be scheduled for those interested in hearing their speeches. When a student listens to his talk, knowing the comments of the instructor regarding it, he is in a good position to recognize his shortcomings and take steps to improve.

THE PERSUASIVE SPEECH

Different types of speeches are designed to achieve different objectives. For example, the objective of one speech may be to entertain, another to inform, another to praise, and another to persuade. Each of these is constructed differently as it is developed to reach its goal.

Use a Bit of Imagination and Psychology

We will concentrate on the speech designed to persuade. Since persuasion is necessary, we may assume the audience is not sympathetic to the issue involved. For this reason, the speech of persuasion must be developed with a bit of imagination and psychology.

The Opening Is Very Important

If the audience is not sympathetic and we open our talk with a statement regarding our objective, we might find ourselves finishing the talk in a rather empty hall. Instead, we must open on a friendly note. Say something pleasant; if you can honestly praise the audience, do so.

Make It Easy for the Audience to Agree with You

Having broken the ice, try to establish rapport with the audience. Consider their background. Try to find something that you and they have in common. Try to get the audience to nod their heads in approval concerning several non-controversial statements that you make. Get them to agree with you on several unimportant points.

Seems as Though We Have Borrowed
from Shakespeare

So far, we have practically duplicated the approach Mark Antony used in persuading the Roman citizenry to adopt his point of view regarding the death of Caesar. This is a sound psychological approach worthy of duplication. of duplication.

Motivation, Examples, Reasons,
Plea for Acceptance

Now that we have lessened the resistance of the audience and we have conditioned them to saying "yes," we proceed to create in them a desire to do what we want them to do. We decide on a way to motivate them and we attempt to do so. We furnish examples to show how others have derived benefit. We provide reasons to show why it is best for them to act in a certain way. Finally, when we have used up all our powers of persuasion, we present to the audience the issue we want them to accept.

THE CARD SPEECH

If you go into any public library to look for a certain book written by a certain author, the best place to search for information is in the card reference file. Here you find thousands upon thousands of cards, each in alphabetical order according to book title or author. Each one contains the information necessary to locate a given book in the library.

Speakers' Card File for Research Material

Like the library, many effective speakers keep a card file. This file is usually broken down according to the subject areas which the speaker handles in his talks. A speaker who specializes in industrial programming might have main categories such as "Administration," "Management," "Supervision," and the like. Within the category of "Administration," the speaker might have dividers reading "Budgeting," "Coordinating," "Directing," "Organizing," "Planning," "Reporting," "Staffing," and so on. Within each of these dividers is a 3 × 5 card bearing facts, quotations, examples, and references that can be used for speeches. All these cards are contained in a section marked "Research Material for Speeches."

File for Speeches Which Have Been Delivered

Another section of the card file can be marked "Speeches Delivered." Again, under the categories of "Administration," "Management," and so on, are dividers reading "Budgeting," "Coordinating," etc. Within each of these dividers can be the card outlines of speeches given on that particular subject by the speaker.

Card Outlines

Notice in the last sentence that we used the term "card outlines." Until now, whenever we referred to a speech outline it was generally assumed that the outline would be placed on sheets of paper. That is the normal technique; however, there is an extremely effective alternative. The speaker can place his outline on cards.

Effective Speaking Card Outline

For example, I used cards for my effective speaking lectures over a period of twenty years. I started out with 3 × 5 cards. After about ten years, they got so filled up and shopworn I replaced them with 4 × 6 cards.

In this outline was one card marked "Introduction," and one marked "Closing Statement." Then there was one set banded together for the *musts*, one set for *don't worries*, one set for *helps*, one set for *avoids*, and one set for *how to improve*. Within these sets there was a card for every item included in the Check List located at the back of this book. For thirteen years at the summer session at St. Lawrence University, this card outline provided me with sufficient material for a fifteen-hour course on effective speaking.

Advantages of Card Outline

Having a separate card for each main point and each supporting point in your speech makes it easy to add material. If an item on the radio, television, stage, motion picture, magazine or newspaper impressed me with its value for effective speaking, I went to my card outline, extracted the appropriate card, made a notation, and returned the enriched card to its proper place. When I looked at Billy Graham's notes through binoculars in Madison Square Garden, I saw notations in pencil, in blue ink, and in red ink. My notations at the end of several years presented the same appearance.

Sequence of Cards Can Be Changed Easily

This card outline is very versatile: It can be rearranged to suit your particular needs. For example, when I conduct an effective speaking course, I start with the "introduction" card, followed by the "Musts" and the "Don't Worries." At this point, I never know which card will be used next! That seems like a ridiculous statement to make; however, after an explanation, you should be additionally impressed with the versatility of the card outline.

Cards Used as Basis for Critiquing Short Talks

After discussing the *don't worries,* I called on individual students for the delivery of a three-minute talk. As each student spoke, I seated myself at the rear of the room with my card outline. As the speech progressed, I observed what the student did well or not so well. I went through my card outline, selected cards relating to these strengths or weaknesses, and then lectured on these cards.

This technique made my comments more meaningful for the student since we covered the points in depth. It was also of great value to the class because they related the points discussed to the real live example they had just seen and heard. When every student had given a speech, I arranged the remaining cards and lectured on the *helps* and *avoids* left over. After a short break we covered the "How to Improve" cards and finished up with the "Closing Statement."

You Need Carry Only the Cards You Need

The card outline for my effective speaking course consists of more than seventy-five cards. It would be unnecessary for me to carry all the cards along with all the audio/visual aids needed to amplify and emphasize their content. Whenever the course begins, I can estimate how many cards will be required for the first session. Only these cards are taken to class along with their training aids. Before each class that follows, I set aside the cards that have been used and select those scheduled for the next session. You might assume that these cards would easily be misplaced or lost when they are separated and shifted during a course. However, experience has proven that the opposite is true. In the twenty years of working with my effective speaking card outline, never has a single card been lost.

A Card Outline Is Excellent for an Accordion Speech

At some time in the future you may suddenly be asked to speak for a longer or shorter time than originally scheduled. With a card outline system, this task presents no great difficulty even though your speech has already been prepared to fit the original time limit.

If you are asked to condense your speech, you merely extract enough cards to accomplish the change. If you must lengthen the speech, you go to the extra cards in your "Research Material" file and select enough additional cards to add the required time.

Card Outline Is Easy to Carry

A card outline for a thirty-minute talk could slip into the inside pocket of your jacket and never make a bulge. On the other hand, if the outline was on conventional-sized paper, it would have to be folded, and possibly damaged, to fit into such a pocket.

Card Outline Is Easy to Review

Now that the outline is in your pocket, you suddenly have an inspiration and you want to alter your speech. You rest your cards on your lap if you are seated, or hold them in your hand if you are standing, and write in the change. If the outline is on paper, such handling may tear your speech.

During your trip to the location where you will speak, you may travel in a bus, subway, or taxi. You may want to use a few minutes to review your notes. With cards this is simple; however, sheets of paper might cause problems.

Now we'll assume that the speech has begun and you wish to move away from the lectern for a few minutes as you continue to speak. With a card outline, you can accomplish this by holding a card in your hand. Because the card is small, it does not create a distraction for the audience. If you tried this with an outline on a sheet of paper, it could be noticed because of its size and it could prove distracting.

Card Outlines for Other Purposes

The size, durability, and versatility of card outlines prompted me to extend their use. My publishing firm has encountered great success in marketing our "Criminal Law Flash Cards," "Supervision Card Course," and "Crime Breakdown Cards."

Although these cards were intended primarily for use by civil service personnel studying for promotion, some lecturers have adopted them as card outlines for speeches. For example, the "Crime Breakdown Cards" diagram all the elements of forty-three major crimes. Any one of these cards can serve as an outline for a speech on a given major crime. All you need is an attention-getting introduction to open the talk and a strong closing statement to end it.

ten

How
to
Improve

We have discussed in detail the essentials of effective speaking relating to speech organization, speech attitudes, speech techniques, the *avoids*, the *don't worries*, and, most important, the *musts*. Now we consider your future development. We must determine how best to apply the principles set forth in this text so that you will make progress toward your goal of becoming an effective speaker.

ACCEPT ALL INVITATIONS TO SPEAK

Of these five words, the most important is "all." If you now determine that you will accept *all* invitations to speak, you will do more for the development of a positive attitude toward speaking than any other resolution you may adopt.

Commit Yourself and You Will Gain Assurance

Until the age of twenty-four, I had never touched a dead body. Like most other people, I was a bit squeamish about such a prospect and was never quite sure whether I could do it. This doubt stemmed from the fact that *I didn't have to* touch dead bodies; I would make the decision only when the need arose.

This changed when I entered the service. When I put on a uniform, I knew that I *would have to* touch dead bodies in the performance of duty. When I *had* to do it, I was amazed at the way I handled myself.

When you resolve to accept *all* invitations to speak, you commit yourself. You now *have to* speak. You will be amazed, as I was, at the assured manner with which you accept a task to which you have unalterably committed yourself.

If It Is Within Your Power, Accept

A more accurate statement of your future attitude toward speaking would be to accept all invitations to speak, if it is within your power to accept them. We add this qualifying statement for the obvious reason that there may be extenuating circumstances that make it impossible for you to accept an invitation. You may be out of town, or scheduled to speak somewhere else, or made unavailable by other valid reasons. As long as it is a valid reason, a declination is in order. In the absence of a valid reason, the invitation should always be accepted.

When a speaking invitation is extended, the unsophisticated recipient starts racking his brain to discover an excuse for refusing the invitation. The wise recipient figures out how he can accept; says, "Yes"; then begins to prepare.

PREPARE SPEECHES YOURSELF

Throughout this text we have emphasized the importance of knowledge. We indicated that the most valuable type of knowledge is that which the speaker has *personally* experienced. In view of this fact, the advantages of preparing a speech yourself are obvious. Self-preparation produces material most interesting for the listener. Because you are familiar with the content of the speech, you derive confidence and improve your delivery.

Self-Preparation Stimulates Sincerity

For you to be most effective, we have stressed the fact that you must believe in your subject. If another person prepares a speech; the individual who delivers it may lack conviction when he speaks someone else's words to the audience. However, if the speaker has produced the content of the talk, it is natural that sincerity will be apparent and impressive.

Self-Preparation Stimulates Enthusiasm

There is a little bit of "ham" in all of us. If you are waving someone else's banner or speaking someone else's speech, you may not do it with much enthusiasm. But, if you are advertising your own product; if you are delivering a message that contains your words, then you are more eager to speak out. Self-preparation encourages abundant enthusiasm.

If Self-Preparation Is Not Possible

We realize that it may be impossible to prepare the speech yourself. In such a case, you should go over the manuscript carefully. You should make changes and additions to improve and personalize the speech. Then, you should give a great deal of effort and attention to rehearsal.

REHEARSE

Never, never, never give a speech without a rehearsal. The importance of rehearsal cannot be overemphasized. There are several things of which you should be aware.

If Possible, Rehearse Where You Will Speak

Ideally, you should rehearse in the room where you will actually deliver the speech. You should have the actual notes of the speech, the lectern, the visual aids, the blackboard and chalk, the lights, the amplification system, the seating arrangement for the audience, and everything else you will use for the actual speech. You should have a few people listening. Have a friend give an introduction if your actual appearance will be introduced. Have your timepiece handy and carefully time your speech as you deliver it.

If You Can't Rehearse "On Location," Rehearse Elsewhere

It will not always be possible to have a rehearsal "on location." If this is the case, rehearse somewhere else— but rehearse. Rehearse in your home, in your office, in your automobile, in any place that guarantees no interruptions for the duration of your talk. In 1964, I was scheduled to give the principal address at a panel discussion at St. Lawrence University moderated by Patrick V. Murphy who was then Chief of the Syracuse Police Department. On my way to Syracuse, I scheduled a stop along the New York State Thruway to rehearse my speech. I pulled off the highway, produced my notes, recorded my starting time, and began to deliver my talk to the trees in front of the car visible through the windshield. There was sincerity, enthusiasm, gestures, and other approved speech techniques. When I was about twenty minutes into the talk, there was a tapping on the window. There stood a State Trooper with a quizzical expression on his face. I hurriedly explained what I was doing, he smilingly wished me luck, and I finished my rehearsal. The speech and the panel discussion were successful. This was due in large measure to sound preparation, which included a forty-five minute rehearsal under State Police supervision.

If Half the Time Spent Worrying Was Given to Rehearsal...

People are inclined to worry about a speech they have to give. Regarding this, I guarantee that if one-half of the time usually spent worrying was given to rehearsal, then there wouldn't be anything to worry about. Next time you begin to tense up before a talk, look at your watch. If you still have enough time for another rehearsal, rehearse! Your time will be well spent, your tenseness will be dissipated in positive action, and your actual delivery will benefit from the additional familiarity and confidence this rehearsal will provide.

APPLY THE PRINCIPLES OF EFFECTIVE SPEAKING

While you are preparing and rehearsing and delivering your speeches in the future, apply the principles of effective speaking.

Use the "Effective Speaking Checklist" Regularly

Make your development as interesting, as meaningful, and as enjoyable as possible. Here is a suggested way to approach your program of self-improvement. For your guidance, we have reproduced an "Effective Speaking Checklist," which begins on page 279. Every time you make a talk, concentrate on one of the checklist techniques such as gestures, pauses, eye contact, volume, and the like. Insert the date, and record any remarks you feel are significant to your effective speaking career. Also, if an incident occurs at any time which relates to any item on the checklist, insert the date and make a note of the details under "Remarks."

If Possible, Make Arrangements So You Will Be Exposed to This Checklist Each Day

Frank Sullivan took our course in 1956. Two years later he told me about a ritual he had developed with the Effective Speaking Checklist he had received during the course. He placed it on the inside of his locker door. While he was changing his clothes, he referred to his checklist and selected the item he would concentrate on during that day's three hours of lectures. He said that the daily appearance of the checklist when he opened his locker served as a challenge. Later in the classroom followed

276

the stimulating and beneficial experience of adding a new technique to his speaking skills.

Use Checklist, Consult Index, Review Pages That Refer to Item, Apply Technique in Next Speech

To achieve the greatest measure of success as an effective speaker, you must expend intelligent effort. You must be constantly aware of the *musts, helps, avoids,* and *don't worries* of effective speaking. Select items from this checklist, go to the index, read the pages that deal with the item selected, then apply the principles of the technique when you give your next talk.

Don't Be Surprised

Don't be surprised if your progress exceeds your expectations. One thing is sure, by applying good effective speaking techniques on a real live audience, you will derive a rich reward. You will know that your words are having an impression on other people's lives. You will experience the deep satisfaction that comes from your sincere attempt to make this impression as meaningful as possible.

CLOSING STATEMENT

Here is the statement I have used to close all my talks and courses in effective speaking since 1954. It is equally as appropriate to the readers of this book as it was in face-to-face contacts with my listeners.

Thank Your Audience, Then
Appeal For Action

"Thank you for giving me the most precious thing that you possess. Something which no amount of money can buy. Something which is in limited supply. Something which cannot be replaced once it is used. Thank you for giving me your life's time.

"In the days and years to come, if each one of you approaches the speaker's platform with a full realization that the audience is giving you the very best that it can offer, then you, in return, cannot help giving the audience the very best speech that you can deliver."

Effective Speaking Checklist

(See page 276 for explanation regarding use of checklist)

	Date	Remarks
"Musts"		
Knowledge	_____	_____
Sincerity	_____	_____
Enthusiasm	_____	_____
Practice	_____	_____
"Don't Worries"		
Accent	_____	_____
Audience Opinion	_____	_____
Audience Participation	_____	_____
Breathing Technique	_____	_____
Education	_____	_____

279

	Date	Remarks
"Er's" and "Ah's"	_____	_____
Nervousness	_____	_____
Shyness	_____	_____
Speaking faults	_____	_____
Vocabulary	_____	_____
Voice	_____	_____

"Helps"

Applause	_____	_____
Be Accurate	_____	_____
Be Confident	_____	_____
Be Conversational	_____	_____
Be Objective	_____	_____
Be Yourself	_____	_____
Charisma	_____	_____
Eliminate Distractions	_____	_____
Embarrassment	_____	_____
Emphasis	_____	_____
Enjoy Speaking	_____	_____
Eye Contact	_____	_____
Facts, Examples, Quotations	_____	_____
Feedback	_____	_____
Food and Water	_____	_____
Gestures	_____	_____

	Date	Remarks
Good Appearance	_____	_____
Good Closing	_____	_____
Good Opening	_____	_____
Humor	_____	_____
Imagination	_____	_____
Inflection and Tone	_____	_____
Know Your Audience	_____	_____
Mnemonic Devices	_____	_____
No Comment	_____	_____
Outline for Speech	_____	_____
Pauses	_____	_____
Posture	_____	_____
Preparation	_____	_____
Questions	_____	_____
Rate	_____	_____
Refer to Locale	_____	_____
Simplicity and Clarity		_____
Situation-Savers	_____	_____
Timing	_____	_____
Use Names	_____	_____
Use Psychology	_____	_____
Visual Aids	_____	_____
Volume	_____	_____
"We's," "You's," "I's"	_____	_____

	Date	Remarks

"Avoids"
Alcohol

Announcing Subject
at Start

Antagonizing Audience

Apologizing for Speech

Dependence on Stories

False Confidence

Grammatical Errors

Holding Lectern

Memorizing

Mispronunciations

Pacing

Playing with Things

Profanity or Vulgarity

"How to Improve"
Accept All Invitations

Apply Principles of
Effective Speaking

Prepare Speeches
Yourself

Rehearse

Index

A

Accent, 41-42
Acceptance speech, 237-38
Accordion speech, 251-53, 267
Accuracy, 94-95, 235
Alcoholic drinks, 178-80
Announcing subject, 180-82
Antagonizing audience, 182-83
Antony, Mark, 47-48, 263
Apologizing for speech, 183-84
Appearance, importance of your, 127-31
Applause, 97-99
Application stage of presentation, 212-14
Applying principles, 276-77
Army, U.S., 7, 64
Attitude, 9 10, 103ff
  before cameras, 245
Audience opinion, 46-50
Audience participation, 91-92, 194

Audience response, 10-11, 195
"Avoids," 165ff

B

Background, related to learning, 202-3
Beecher, Henry Ward, 20
Being yourself, 108-9
Bernstein, Leonard, 67, 92
Blackboard, use of, 159, 209
"BOM" method, 77, 159, 181-82, 207
Brainstorming, 260
Breathing, 50-51
Brevity, 226, 235
"Bull's Eye of Instruction," 79

C

Card outlines, 264-68
Cards for notes, 263-68